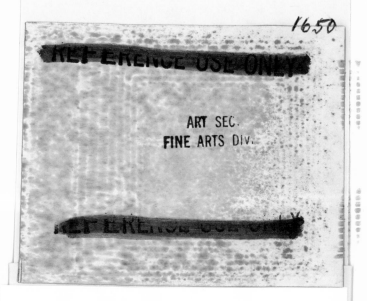

Tales of the

YIDDISH RIALTO

Other works by Louis Lipsky:

A Gallery of Zionist Profiles (1956)

Selected Works of Louis Lipsky, 3 vols. (1927)
    Vol. I—*Thirty Years of American Zionism*
    Vol. II—*Stories of Jewish Life*
    Vol. III—*Shields of Honor: Plays*

Tales of the
YIDDISH RIALTO

**Reminiscences of Playwrights and Players in
New York's Jewish Theatre in the Early 1900's**

By

Louis Lipsky

GREENWOOD PRESS, PUBLISHERS
WESTPORT, CONNECTICUT

Library of Congress Cataloging in Publication Data

Lipsky, Louis, 1876-1963.
   Tales of the Yiddish Rialto.

   Reprint of the 1962 ed. published by T. Yoseloff,
New York.
   1. Theater--Jews--Anecdotes, facetiae, satire, etc.
2. Theater--New York (City)--Anecdotes, facetiae,
satire, etc. I. Title.
[PN3035.L49 1977]   792'.09747'1   77-7895
ISBN 0-8371-9681-7

c.1

© 1962 by A. S. Barnes and Company, Inc.

Originally published in 1962 by Thomas Yoseloff, New York.

Reprinted with the permission of A.S. Barnes & Company, Inc.

Reprinted in 1977 by Greenwood Press, Inc.

Library of Congress Catalog Card Number 77-7895

ISBN 0-8371-9681-7

Printed in the United States of America

This book is dedicated to
the one who inspired
my love for the Yiddish Theater—
"Eddie," mother of my three sons.

AUTHOR'S NOTE

It would be futile to pretend that these characters from the Yiddish Rialto are figments of my imagination. Any resemblance between them and real people is entirely inevitable.

Jacob Adler, Bertha Kalich, Kenia Lipzin, David Kessler, Sarah Adler, Sigmund Mogulescu, Jacob Gordin, Morris Moscowitch, and a host of others—they are all there, every one.

But I thought it only fitting to their profession to disguise them, and to alternate their roles as the fancy took me.

So they are still playing a part. It will be up to the historian to determine who has been cast in which role, but I hope the reader will be satisfied in the knowledge that the actors are as real as their make-up.

Louis Lipsky
New York City, 1962

CONTENTS

PROLOGUE

THESE STORIES—IF THEY MAY BE CALLED THAT—ARE ABOUT
mountebanks, or even troubadours. The scene is the East
Side of New York, about fifty years ago. Mountebanks they
certainly were, but it may be far-fetched to say that the men
and women strutting through these pages were troubadours.
What would a troubadour be doing in the crowded streets of
the East Side? And a Jewish troubadour at that! His voice
would have been drowned in the noises of the street, by the
drone that came from the many places of worship, by the
noisy haggling of the merchants and their customers on
Baxter Street. The singing of a lyric song, à la troubadour,
was unknown. They were vagrants who had become actors
and singers in a theatre.

They lived in the Ghetto but were not part of it. They
mocked its ways. They knew the conventions, but laughingly
violated them. Their marriages were not registered in heaven,
for they even exchanged partners without the intervention
of a rabbi; they were sharpers and rogues even in their love-
making. What they played on the stage was the usual make-
believe. And that make-believe was consciously transferred
to the street, in a different style. The street—that was the
place for posing in three dimensions. The street was for the
show of gaudy clothes, the twirling of a cane, the wearing of
high hat or dashing fedora, the heavy gold watch chain and

11

the glittering diamond ring (bought for a rainy day, with an
eye on the pawnshop close by), and the pompous strut. There
was something unreal in their appearance, as though mas-
queraders had mistaken the hour and wandered into broad
daylight with their masks on. It was as if a distinctive uniform had been donned for street wear, different only in kind
from the strange trappings of the stage, but just as artificial
and fantastic.

With few exceptions, the players had the intellect of their
class and profession. (All actors are intellectually peculiar.)
Their brains had been washed clean, as it were, and a smooth,
impressionable surface remained—a *tabula rasa*. Write on
it what you please; the scrawl could easily be erased. The
text of one role obliterated its predecessor. They used words
glibly, fluently, and seemed to be listening to the sound of
their voices, pleased; but what the words signified was matter
beyond their ken. They would join a conversation eagerly
(like docile pupils, willing to learn), but you felt that a light-
hearted impertinent sprite fluttered about the ideas that were
being aired and never landed flatly on the spot. They would
become warm and excited, would pretend to be engrossed,
but their warmth and enthusiasm were provoked by the
artist's interest in disputatious exercise; they wanted to be
in the center of that stage, too. Their interest was in the
excitement, and in the technique of expressing it; but the
cause of the excitement, the heart of the matter, was irrelevant. "How well he talks," the febrile Mme. Lessin would
say, and immediately tackle the outer circle of listeners in
order gradually to worm herself into a place of distinction.
She liked to be seen in the midst of an intellectual discussion.
"What a mouth he has, and what a head," the grandiose
Alexander Ritter would exclaim, as a colleague spun out an
intricate argument; and he would at once begin to ponder

what he was going to say as soon as he could find an opening. He admired the loquacity of the speaker, the choice words that were used, the sound of his voice, the ease with which expression was achieved; but only in the way of comparison. How much better he could do it; please give him the floor!

They did not have the satisfaction of creating their own world of make-believe, for even their plays did not belong to them. Except for a few Biblical and legendary melodramas and operettas, the pieces in which they appeared were for the most part plagiarized. The ballads came from the dim past or, reduced to a minor key, were transported from the *opéras comiques* or the music-halls of other peoples. Lacking original playwrights of their own, they had to resort to the pirating of plays, disguising the *dramatis personae* of the original dramas and overlaying them with the qualities and the idiom of Jews. (These plagiarized compositions were never discovered by their original authors, for who in the outer world knew of the existence of the Yiddish Rialto?) They also drew upon the history of the Jews in Spain, but all plays of this genre were mere replicas. They laid hold of Schiller—"Don Carlos" and "The Robbers"—and a few of the tragedies of a later day. "Monte Cristo" was a popular melodrama. The Jewish strain was derived from the Purim play, from remnants of folklore, and from the works of Goldfaden, who was so adept in disguising his sources that he was forever regarded as the creator of the Yiddish drama. But for plays reflecting the contemporaneous Jewish life, there were no playwrights until the arrival of Jacob Gordin, who figures in this volume as Manewitz. He was the first man of intellect and education to intrude into the Yiddish theatre; he bullied his way into prominence. He was a liberal adapter, too, but his standards were lofty. Grillparzer and Hauptmann, and Russian dramatists of whom the Jews of New York had never heard, were his models; he paraphrased in a Jewish setting the plays of greater dramatists. He professed great admiration for Ibsen, then the dramatist of revolt. Gordin strained hard to be a realist, but he was by nature a sketch-writer, and spent himself in drawing characters who were always patterned to fit the actors for whom he was writing.

With Gordin came several lesser lights, like Leon Kobrin and Z. Libin, who, striving to share Gordin's glory, feebly disputed his reign, but failed for lack of vigor and imagination to make a deep impression upon their time. A fresher, more original spirit came into the Yiddish theatre after Gordin crumpled up and died. The Yiddish theatre I knew died with Gordin.

In the early days, there was no genuine Yiddish drama, and it may be added, not even a validated language in the Yiddish theatre. The language they used was a composite of all the Jewish languages of a long-drawn-out exile. There were ninety and nine Yiddish dialects. What was the core of the language? That was for you to find out! All the Jewries of the world had contributed to the personnel of the theatre; and when they reached the East Side and met in one dramatic company, they first used a quaintly pompous German, which they thought all could speak, more or less. (For all Jews were presumed to have a nodding acquaintance with German.) It was a language of sonority, fit for classical declamation. For a time, authentic Yiddish—whatever it was—was unknown on the stage. The pronunciation of Yiddish varied with the player. For many years some of the leading players refused to abandon German. That was a language, they said, your teeth could bite into. They thought Yiddish was vulgar. If you had a lord or a priest in a play, how in Heaven's name could you have him speak the language of the kitchen? Give aristocrats German; let the lout come on the stage and speak

Yiddish. That was fitting. Yiddish was—frankly speaking—
the language of the servant girl and of workmen. When,
finally, Yiddish had its literary development in the old country, and had to be admitted into the Temples of Art on the
East Side, the players quarreled over the right pronunciation.
Which should prevail—the Yiddish of Lithuania (but that
was a guttural dialect) or the Yiddish of Poland (but that was
too thin) or of the Odessa region? (Now that had style and
heft to it!) Eventually a form of Yiddish was adopted by common consent, but what was used was really a contrived language, subject to the vagaries of actors and playwrights. Years
after Gordin's death, the Yiddish of Peretz, Sholom Aleichem,
David Pinski, and Sholom Asch was given place in the Yiddish theatre. It was hard on the old actors, but the changes
time effects are always cruel to those who overstay their
welcome.

They seldom crossed the line; they remained within their
own precinct. They had their own coffee-houses and restaurants, their own gambling places, their own billiard and pool
rooms. Within the four walls of their club-rooms the outer
world was never admitted. They spoke of their patrons as
aliens. What did they, the *Moshes*, know of theatre? They
were so easily beguiled and entertained. It was a rabble.
Burlak of the stentorian voice once walked down to the
footlights and addressed the gallery gods as follows: "You
zhulikes, haven't you got manners? When an actor talks, the
gallery should hold its tongue." Once in a while a bold merchant, having accumulated a few thousand dollars, would
essay the role of theatrical angel. He would find a manager
to accommodate him. But when the angel came to see the
actor or manager in his favorite coffee-house, he was made to
feel that he was being received on sufferance. It was their
theatre. Their audiences were favored or privileged people.

They were tolerated. The box office, you understand, but
what other use do they serve? Can you rely upon their judgment? Do they come to see the best plays—the plays in which
I rant about the stage in a vigorous manner, tear a passion
to tatters, show what I can do? An ignorant, gullible rabble!
The actors had their own manner of speech, their own manner of dress, their own manner of eating—breakfast when
others were eating lunch, lunch when others were eating dinner, dinner when others were going to sleep. They had their
own vulgarities and indecencies—guzzling, gorging, fornicating—a motley assortment.

Make-believe—on the stage and off!
But what was behind the pose and the pretense? Where
was the soul of these mountebanks? Did they never peel off
the pretensions, remove the grease paint, efface the veneer,
and show themselves as human beings, sans the trappings of
their mockeries? All these outer garments, and not a glimpse
of the core! All this froth and tittle-tattle, these gyrations and
tactics, and not a sign of the manipulator of the puppet's
strings! Quit your mouthings and grimaces; let's see your own
authentic face, the tongue that does not lie, the eye that looks
at you straight, the hand that touches with a natural warmth!
The real and the pose were so mixed that they could not be
separated. Even when they were on the verge of death you
could not tell whether they were behaving as real persons, or
simply showing off to the Angel of Death.

I have tried to give a glimpse, here and there, into the
reality in their hocus-pocus, the truth in their make-believe.
Scarcely a trace of the world in which they lived is now left.
It has passed away and another layer of life has been deposited
above it. May your eyes see what I have attempted to bring
to life again with understanding and a forgiving spirit.

Tales of the
YIDDISH RIALTO

I

The Circle of a Life

A THOUSAND EYES GLARED AT HIM FROM THE GALLERY. A FEW hundred faces stared from the orchestra seats. The heat wrapped itself around him like a blanket. He felt like throwing off his boots and the heavy overcoat, which were part of the costume in the role he was playing; or at least ripping open the collar which was choking him.

He was a tired old man, and he had played many, many parts. He would have liked to sit down in the wings and rest a while; but his legs were rooted to the stage, and there he had to stand. It was so ordained. In that brief ultimate moment, his life passed before his eyes like a swift-moving picture. A turning wheel ending where it had begun, and all between was a jumbled, whirling mixture of fragments of color and smells, of pain and joy; many climates, many lands, many cities; all tapering down to the point where he stood—grease paint, a beard, boots, and a heavy overcoat; a father called upon to witness the tragedy of his daughter's life.

19

Far off in the distance—would he ever see it again?—was the great metropolis on the other side of the Atlantic. From Odessa to New York, from New York to Odessa. He was a young man again, and all that had transpired in between was an interlude. Once New York had greeted him with loud applause, and Odessa had been forgotten. Now, Odessa gave him shouts of approval, and New York was a silhouette of the past. He had lived between the two points: crooning and ranting, king and jester, rich man and poor man, tragedy and comedy—and here he was again, a worn-out hulk, a broken-down imitation of a man.

"When will I come to the end of this wretched part?" he muttered.

Odessa!

A frowzy restaurant with waiters so intimate with their clients that they could ask them where they had spent the night, or how much money they had in their pockets. The great Goldfaden sat at a table, rapping for service, endlessly drinking tea. Here he was king. He had created a new diversion, a new interest, and homage was his due. He had hammered together a platform in a beer garden, hung a curtain between the platform and the tables, painted a few drops, set up a few footlights; and that platform he had transformed into a Yiddish theatre. He had made it live with singing puppets, with strutting heroes and weeping heroines, with kings and villains, with grand inquisitors and dancing servants. They were plays he had stolen from French comedies, from Grillparzer and Schiller; historical plays from Jewish tradition; melodies from Offenbach; jokes picked up from the gutters of Paris and Vienna and Bucharest. But all of it he had made himself, and he was proud of his creation. The Jews pushing into the capital after the Turkish War owed him royalties they would be having to pay for the rest of his life. But it was a hard struggle, just then, to collect what they already owed him.

The young Dikman, short and stocky, approached the royal presence and with deference mentioned the shape of his ambition. He had come on from a near-by village, where he was a chorister; his shoes were still filled with gravel and covered with mud. His hair was tousled and his eyes hungry, and he looked at Goldfaden appealingly. The composer of "Shulamith" put a few serious questions to him, ordered him to sing a well-known ballad, scrutinized him from head to foot through his glasses, and finally nodded his approval. He would take this yokel as a pupil, but he warned him of the hardships that would face him. They were all artists and had to be prepared to suffer for their art. Suffering was the badge of all their tribe, but they were hoping for better days. There was no money in it, but he assured Dikman that he need not starve.

Without hesitation the young man entered into the spirit of the mimic world which he was doomed never to leave. He sang the songs Goldfaden wrote, spouted rhymed verse with gusto, learned the art of make-up, and was patted on the back by the dramatist and manager. But Dikman fumbled in his empty pockets and felt his stomach. He was as hungry as a ravenous wolf. What was the good of Fame when the stomach had nothing in it? When he suggested payment on account, Goldfaden was infuriated and drew himself up, prepared to lash him on the spot. He held himself in check, however, and mentioned a part in a new play which would be the making of an actor.

"But a good part gives me no bread to eat," said Dikman.

"Is art nothing to you?" exclaimed Goldfaden. "What were you when I took you in? A country yokel, an ignoramus, an upstart lout, did not know how or where to stand, with no grace, no presence, no voice. What are you today? You are an actor, the same as Sonnenthal. You know how to sing the ballads I write. You declaim the words uttered by kings and princes and inquisitors. You are a duelist and a dancer. You know how to stand and you know how to fall. But money—where do they make it, and what has it to do with art, anyway?"

Goldfaden was then living in a well-furnished apartment, and he did himself well. His credit at the restaurant adjoining the theatre was unrestricted. The actors attracted people to the restaurant. At the same time, Goldfaden felt that he had to keep rebellion down. But Dikman was a dull sort of a fellow. He was phlegmatic. He did not know how to turn a corner in diplomacy. He had no reply for Goldfaden and decided that his only way out was to leave. He packed his meagre belongings and left for Rumania. He was in the nick of time. The Yiddish theatre in Odessa got into political difficulties. A scrimmage between Goldfaden and a rival manager aroused the attention of the police. There were denunciations. The police were supposed not to know anything about the existence of the Yiddish theatre, but once their eyes were officially opened to the audacious behavior of Jews fighting in the street, they closed both theatres. For a decade the Yiddish theatre was banished from Russia.

But matters were no better in Bucharest, with its brawling soldiery, the excitement of release from the depressions of the war, and the disdain of the better classes for the vulgarities of the Yiddish theatre. Dikman found a company of hungry, quarreling players. The quarrels arose from the introduction of young women as members of the company. They were called in to take the places of young men who were no longer fit to impersonate women. Some of the so-called actresses were recruited from the local brothels. They brought with them auxiliary vices theretofore unknown to

the men. What resulted was a shocking spectacle full of
complications. Sodom and Gomorrah were often mentioned,
and the actors were reduced to the level of camp-followers
and pickpockets. Time and again the communal fathers were
on the verge of having them kicked out of town. They were
deterred by the fear of blackening the Jewish name, so to
speak, in the eyes of non-Jews. Dikman kept himself free
from the lures of the Delilahs of the company; he was too
stolid to give way to temptation; he despised promiscuity
and vice; at that time he was still under the sway of the
traditions of the village in which he had been born, and
could not reconcile the heroic Bar Kochba (whom he
played) and the conniving Lotharios who used their women
as sources of pocket-money and for enhancing their value
in the theatre in the eyes of servant girls in the galleries.
But Bucharest served to give Dikman self-assurance and a
feeling of superiority. Without waiting for the theatre to
sink to its lowest level, but alarmed at the prospect of
competition from the many actors coming from their exile
in Russia, Dikman was again forced to make a decision. He
always evaded struggle and combat, but he never hesitated
to act. Again he packed his valise and left for England.

The great metropolis of the British Empire was limited,
in Dikman's eyes, to the area in the vicinity of Whitechapel,
the old theatre on Mile End Road, and the Jewish restaurant
near the Aldgate pump. That was where he lived. That was
England and the British Empire. He never saw beyond that.
He found his way to a coterie of actors, and soon became
one of the leading players of the company. Performances
could be given only on weekends. Dikman brought with him
a number of novelties in the way of plays, and of course
took the better parts for himself. It was in London that he
first met Ritter.

Every man is entitled to at least one good hate. It serves

to drain the sadistic impulses that are to be found in every human being, the vestigial dross of primitive savagery. Dikman hated Ritter, at first for no good reason. It was a hate nurtured by the experiences of many years. Ritter came from Odessa. He was tall and handsome. He could not sing; he was not a comedian, nor was he made for heroic parts; he had not yet struck his métier. But he was distinguished as a libertine, charming, bold, and heartless. He was impartial in his amorous adventures, taking up with working girls, or staid wives of shopkeepers, or actresses of the company. He was gay and irresponsible. He was the exact opposite of Dikman, who hated him just for that.

The hero in the Yiddish theatre, at that time, had to be a versatile figure, capable of raising his voice in song. The day of the character actor had not come. Nor was the Hamlet type yet known. It was the heyday of the heroic, the big in everything. Beards had to be worn, and long gabardines. There was little introspection. Whatever was in the lung had to come out on the tongue, as the saying goes. That was the day just suited for Dikman. There was really no need for him to hate Ritter, for there was no rivalry between them. But when the stocky Dikman saw the lithe and laughing Ritter walk down the street, twirling a cane, looking about him eagerly for smiling and welcoming faces, Dikman thought: "I don't know why, but I just hate his guts."

In the measure his heart hardened toward Ritter, it did the reverse toward a young actress, Dinah Rosen. She attracted flocks of young businessmen to the theatre. She pranced about the stage in song and dance, bubbling over with good spirits. She seemed willing to let Dikman fall head over heels in love with her. In fact, she seemed to invite a general assault on her virtue, and her success in the theatre was measured by the number of victims dangling after her. She was too quick for Dikman, and parried his attacks with great skill. He was too dull to feel the contempt in her voice when he allowed himself to be directed from his purpose by her facile repartee. But he kept in pursuit with dogged persistence. The more she eluded him, the more determined he was to follow.

He made rapid strides in his profession. He followed his bent for melodrama by having adaptations made of "Othello," Schiller's "Robbers," and Gutzkow's "Uriel Acosta." He bellowed his way through these heavy pieces and set the fashion for plays in which the "prose" could be chewed and delivered at the audience with a resounding smack. He loved to see himself in tights, or, rather, to feel himself in them; he filled them so snugly and felt so comfortable in them.

But the greater his success, the more disaffected the company became. There had been created a sort of guild equality among the players; the profits were shared; there were no stars; the faces of all the actors appeared in the same size on the posters that were used to decorate the shop-windows. But you could not play Othello for long without having the Moor stick in the eyes of all who saw the play. Nor could Uriel Acosta be made to appear as one of the members of an ensemble. Whoever played Uriel Acosta inevitably became the star.

What Ritter lacked as an actor, he made up for with his bent as an intriguant. He was a clever rogue. He set in motion a conspiracy against Dikman, which made his life insufferable. The players missed their cues; they interfered with his soliloquies; they volunteered original comments on his playing while standing with him on the stage; they marred his declamatory climaxes with coughs and whispers.

Dikman called Ritter aside one morning at rehearsal, and

said, "You *loksh,* how long is this going to keep on?"

"As long as you want to be the only cabbage in the patch," said Ritter.

As I have said, Dikman was incapable of organized resistance. Nor could he resist the cabal formed against him. He always saw one way out of his predicament: retreat. He was a man of quick decision, and once things became too uncomfortable he could not resist the impulse to run away. He brought to life a hidden desire, and went to see Dinah in her dingy lodgings. He said to her:

"The climax of my career I have reached in London. I can get no further because of the envy of these *purtzes* I am condemned to play with. I must find other worlds to conquer."

"What have I to do with these new worlds?" she said.

"I take you into all my plans," he said.

"What do you mean?" she asked, offended.

"I want you to marry me and go with me to America," he replied. "With a partner—young, attractive, a good soubrette—we can make theatre history in New York."

The young woman arose and said coolly:

"I am not in the marrying mood. Nor am I the marrying kind—yet. So don't bother me."

"I am sorry," he said, his head bowed. "But won't you go with me anyway?"

"I'll do one thing: I'll file your application for reference," she said as she dismissed him.

But Dikman had no time to waste on sentiment, nor would he allow this disappointment to influence his decision. An adventure in a strange country would have been less disagreeable in her company, but he would go without her. He was able to replace one pleasure with another. He packed his belongings, took with him the manuscripts of his plays, and said goodby with an exaggerated outburst of sentiment to his fellow actors. He looked at Ritter sourly and said: "I hope I never see your ugly face again."

For two reasons Dikman had the field to himself, swelling up in the free air of the new democracy. He strutted among the actors, looking down on them, for he brought with him tales of successes in Odessa, Bucharest, and London. He was a star from the other side, which still remained the mother country. His girth expanded, for he ate well. He walked with a swagger, as he remembered Ritter had walked. He bought a fur coat and flashed a diamond ring. He was the cock of the walk. But these sweet waters were soon made sour by the exiled players from the other side, as one by one they descended upon the East Side and made themselves at home in the land of Columbus. A second company was formed. There was great excitement and competition, but that was the period of expansion, the period of the great Jewish immigration, and there seemed to be room for all.

Among the first arrivals was Ritter, not so youthful, bronzed by the sea voyage and more serious. When Dikman heard that there was a wife with him, he burst out laughing and said to Simonov, the actor of old men's parts: "This must be a joke."

"Not at all," said Simonov. "He is really married and taken up with her, and there is a child, too."

"That's rich," said Dikman.

Madame Ritter turned out to be Dinah Rosen. She came with her husband to see Dikman soon after their arrival, and when she held out her plump hand there was uncommon warmth in its pressure. Dikman looked at her out of the corner of his eye. She was prettier but stout, and she had grown serious in speech and more sedate in manner.

"Can't we make some arrangement?" asked Ritter.

"What do you mean?" said Dikman.

"We haven't come here to make shoes," said Ritter.

The old grudge Dikman bore him boiled to the point of angry explosion, but he controlled himself and said: "I welcome you both. Make yourself at home. You can have the freedom of the city. As far as playing is concerned, I'll let you have the theatre for three performances next week, in your own repertoire. If the audiences like you, we'll talk about this again."

They made quite a furore. Ritter had developed several good character parts and was now an excellent player; and Dinah had ceased her prancing and singing and was a fairly good actress in emotional roles. The envy went out of Dikman, for he was delighted with the new Dinah, with whom playing together in the same company now brought him into close companionship. Although he was a father, Ritter seemed to pay no further attention to his wife. He was a man who hated the conventional. The shackles of domesticity never bound him. All his promises were made subject to discount and repudiation. But this promise had no validity at all; the shackles of matrimony fell from him like handcuffs from the wrists of Houdini.

The system of profit-sharing still prevailed in the Yiddish theatre. Members of the company received as wages a certain percentage of the weekly profits. That did not mean that all the players were equal. There were grades based on experience, distinctions among the parts; but once the percentage was fixed, it continued during the entire season. When Ritter arrived Dikman had been, in effect, the leading actor. Ritter soon achieved a position second to his. But unlike Ritter, Dikman had no head for business. The younger actor had been a bookkeeper in Odessa, before he ran away to the theatre. There was order even in his amours. He

had a feeling for balance in accounts. Thus, although Dikman received more money each week, Ritter always seemed
more affluent. Ritter seemed a profligate, but was not. Dikman gave the impression of a hard-headed merchant, but
was capable of ruinous extravagance in the theatre.

Who provoked the climax—Dikman or Madame Ritter—
it is hard to say. But Dikman was driven to declare himself
with a fervor and a passion not his habit. When he sat
opposite Dinah in the café one evening, he recalled what
she had said in London—that she would file his application
for future reference. She was now estranged from her husband. There was a buxom maid to care for the child. She
acted in her husband's repertoire, but she was as free as if
she had been unmarried. By now, Dikman regarded Ritter
as the enemy of his life. Ritter had not only jostled him
off the stage in London, but threatened the same procedure
in New York. He had taken from him the only woman for
whom he had a lasting regard. He was determined that the
first act of revenge would be to recover possession of Dinah.
Everything, he thought, moved toward that heartless scoundrel. Ritter attracted so many women; money coming into
his pocket stuck there. There was a frugality even in his
movements on the stage. He made hit after hit with parts
other actors had discarded. He grew by leaps and bounds in
public esteem, and there was something exotic and grand
in his manner, something strangely attractive in the pictures
displayed of him on the posters. Why should I not take his
wife away from him? ruminated Dikman. He threw discretion to the winds.

Dinah was led astray—if that is the right word to use—
not so much by love for Dikman as anger toward Ritter.
She felt that he had in mind to reduce her to the position
of a housewife, or a nurse-maid; that he did not relish play-

ing with her in the same repertoire. She knew that it
cramped his style to feel her watchful eye upon him while
they were playing. She resented Ritter's advancement, with
which she could not keep pace. On the other hand, Dikman showered her with attention, gave her a good time
whenever she craved it, and treated her like a comrade. She
felt more at home in his company.

The course of their love was beset with deception, nervous excitement, tantrums, and, as their mutual passion waxed
strong, they lost caution and modesty in public behavior,
and it soon became common gossip that the House of Ritter
was about to suffer a stroke.

As usual, Dikman shrank from the collision which seemed
imminent. He hated scenes and struggle. The matter was
taken out of his hands, however, by Ritter himself, who
suddenly began to take a lively interest in the affair as if it
were developing in line with a scenario he had written. Not
by word or gesture did the betrayed husband intimate his
suspicions to either his wife or her lover. They were made
to feel that they had least to fear from him. They were lulled
into a sense of security. Thus the denouement came com-
pletely without warning. Their rendezvous having been observed by a man whom Ritter had engaged, they were discovered and confronted in a shabby West Side hotel room.
Ritter gave a splendid impersonation of a deceived husband;
he had played the part time and again. He breathed fire and
shed tears.

"What are you going to do about it?" asked Dikman de-
fiantly. His triumph was not as he imagined it would be.
His position was again inferior to Ritter's who had the
center of the stage. It seemed that he was always destined to
play the stooge wherever Ritter was concerned. He had expected to laugh in Ritter's face, taunt him a bit, and stride

off the scene in triumph. Instead, Dinah stood in a corner of the room adjusting her costume, powdering her nose, a curiously mocking look in her eyes, as if she were witnessing the rehearsal of a scene in which she had nothing to do at the moment.

"And I tell you I am going to divorce this jade," said Ritter, "and nothing will stop me."

"That's what I have been wanting you to do for a long time," said Dikman.

"And I'll tell you this: If you don't marry her," said Ritter, "I'll break every bone in your fat carcass. I won't stand for any nonsense from you."

"She should have married me in the first place," said Dikman, "and as to breaking bones, I'll have something to say about that."

But it was Ritter who strode out of the scene, the detective at his heels. He felt that he had disposed of the matter gracefully. Why should the betrayed husband be ugly in such a situation? Good riddance. Take it calmly. What have I lost? Hereafter Dikman would have to provide for his mistress, not he. He had his own affairs to think of.

"I shall marry you on one condition," said Dinah after Ritter had left.

"Anything to please you, my dear," said Dikman sullenly.

"I want always to act with you in the same company," she said. "I don't want to trail after you like a scullion. We are partners and I want to be treated like an equal."

"Agreed," said Dikman.

That promise was his nemesis.

There was a divorce. The issue was the custody of the child. Ritter had a liking for children. Not when they were infants and troublesome, but when they were beginning to be persons. It was said that he had left remembrances of

himself in many cities, who later in life presented themselves to their putative father and were accepted without
protest or demur. He would take a good look at any boy
or girl who came to have him acknowledge his parenthood,
and if the look satisfied him, that sealed the relationship.
But rather than prolong the affair with Dinah, and dread-
ing a public disclosure of his life in any investigation of
his fitness to care for the child, he magnanimously resigned
the child to Dinah's care and pretended to be heartbroken.

Dikman suffered no loss of prestige, and later accepted
an engagement to play in Burlak's company. Dinah was to
play with him. When Dikman thought of the whole incident, he realized the defeat he had suffered. He had taken
over a wife and child discarded by Ritter. While Dikman
had been immersed in his guilty passion, Ritter had moved
ahead. He had brought the profit-sharing system to an end.
He was in a position to purchase the lease of the theatre
in his own name. He had acquired an ambitious East Side
business man as his partner. As a result, the following season
the actors had to be engaged by Ritter as lessee, who offered
them fixed salaries above their earnings the previous year.
They were children in practical matters. They were satisfied until they discovered that they had been deprived of
their patrimony. They were no longer equals in a system
based upon merit and service. They were acting for a manager. They were wage-slaves. That was the beginning of the
actors' union. Once the wage system was accepted in Ritter's theatre, it had to be set up in the other Yiddish theatres.

In this economic revolution Dikman was hard hit. The
shuffling of the cards moved him from the top of the pack.
He might have been a star in other days, but his face on the
posters suffered a reduction in size that made his inferiority
apparent to all observers. He still had his own repertoire,

but the plays had become dated. Dikman and his wife received wages like the other players and were billed as stars, but this pretense had no practical value. In addition, Dikman had put on weight. His face became heavy and flabby. His voice was now like the groaning of a cider barrel. He could not be the hero any longer. He was too fat. Dinah shared in his alarm and advised seeking the counsel of a dietitian, but Dikman attributed all his difficulties to the manager, the robust Burlak, who—in Dikman's view—was afraid of a rival and was determined to keep him down. What had his weight to do with his acting? He was just as good an actor now as he ever was. How about Possart's size? Possart too looked like a beer barrel. And what about others he could mention. not to speak of Burlak himself?

Dikman and Burlak soon had a disagreement that congealed into frigid animosity, and Dikman gave his manager a final scowl and left the theatre. He could now either set up a theatre of his own or capitulate to Ritter. As he had no money and there was no "angel" in sight, eating dirt, as he said, was the only alternative. Guessing that Dikman would remain true to his bovine nature, Ritter sent his agent, Lonkes, to the fallen star to negotiate. Lonkes was amiable and generous, but Dikman hesitated as he mentioned his wife.

"Don't be a fool," said Lonkes pleasantly. "Ritter is an artist first and last. Bring Dinah with you."

Ritter took a queer way of showing that he bore no grudge. He ordered Dikman's repertoire taken off the list of benefit plays, and in the first production Dikman appeared with the beard of a patriarch; but he had to swallow his pride and not protest, for Dinah, on the other hand, had been treated with great consideration. Her talents hovered between those of a soubrette and of an emotional actress. She

was not so dainty and not so pert, but that was the sacrifice
Ritter made for old times' sake. Not to be unchivalrous,
Dinah was now a pleasant-faced matron. Her health was
good, her form was not so bad, and she was always vivacious.
When you heard her speak, you did not have to think of
beauty of figure or features.

Dikman vented his anger, sullenly, on his wife. He was
pleased that she was still appreciated by others. To him she
was as good-looking as ever. But his own displacement made
him angry and depressed. Dinah listened to his complaints
with compassion. He was so loyal beneath his gruffness. He
never begrudged her a moment of pleasure. He did not
pursue her with eyes of jealousy. For him she maintained
a steady marital affection. She was no longer so excitable in
a sexual way, and his steadiness served to stabilize her own
truant nature.

Finally, Dikman confessed he could endure the situation
no longer. The oppression of Ritter made life impossible.
He would have to leave. The world was divided into as
many parts as there were Yiddish theatre centers. He thought
of the Argentine. A Jewish settlement had grown up there
out of a colonization scheme financed by a Jewish philan-
thropist. The colonists, instead of remaining on their farms,
drifted toward the capital city, Buenos Aires. They had
thrift and business experience, and soon they had established
newspapers and a Yiddish theatre. But Dikman now lacked
the fire of adventure, and did not go to Buenos Aires. He
took the easier path and went to London. He knew that
Dinah would be a handicap; he needed a fresh, young leading lady; had he dared, he would have proposed going alone,
but since he was rather afraid of her, he did not have the
heart to do it. He felt that she knew his secret, that he was
still jealous of Ritter, and he did not want to desert her

now. She was as necessary to him as the meals he ate with such avidity.

The London Ghetto was a sordid duplicate of the East Side of New York. It lacked the brightness and animation of the New World. It was frowzy and poor. The Jews in London were exiles who would have gone on their way across the Atlantic to join their more fortunate brethren in a new world which they were helping to create, but had been detoured by accidents. In London they lived in the back alley of a city set in its ways, which regarded all aliens as "outsiders" incapable of ever becoming Englishmen. The Statue of Liberty was a symbol that had a meaning—at that time; it extended a hand of welcome and made the alien feel at home. New York was a city of change. You could speak English there with no respect for it. You could maintain your own habits. London was quite different. The weaker exiles from Russia and Poland remained in London. They had their learned men, they had their synagogues and schools; but there were so many hurdles to jump before they could feel at home. That sense of inferiority was reflected in their whole life. They looked up to the Englishman, and they got accustomed to the idea of looking up. They looked up to the Jews coming from Russia, as well as to the Jews coming from "golden" America. They were living in a land of snobs, and inferiority was fixed upon them.

By the little sheet that pretended it was a Yiddish newspaper Dikman was hailed as the greatest tragedian of the Yiddish theatre. A few clubs gave him a reception, at which they served cold tea and cakes. When he walked down Mile End Road, urchins greeted him, and shopkeepers peered out at him. A Yiddish actor walking the street was a novelty. Still, they did not come to see him play. But he remained in spite of difficulties, lived frugally, and waited for that appreciation which—his friends told him—took a long time in coming in London, but which, when it came, abided. Just as the tide seemed to be turning, his nemesis caught up with him. Ritter came to London with a few selected players and made a sensation in the theatre and on the street. For Ritter by this time had acquired a personality which could not be disguised, even when he appeared in street clothes. He was now an imposing fellow. He always wore a tall hat and affected a monocle. His face was fixed in a patrician mold, and he gave the impression of being a distinguished gentleman. On the stage, too, he used mannerisms, spasmodic gestures, lighting effects to bring out his profile, that reminded London Jews of Henry Irving. He gave attention to details of stage business—and had no voice worth mentioning. Dikman was in despair. He threw up his hands and confessed that he could not stand it. He was ruined. He was doomed not to have one full year of peace. The scoundrel seemed to be hounding him. He folded his tents and stole away in the night. He now made his way to the Argentine.

On board the ship he raged and threatened suicide, as he gave vent to his desperation. He reproached Fate and Dinah. But the more he reproached her, the more she clung to him. Kindness had once made her mutinous. Now, her love thrived on unkindness. Her husband said he hated her for her lost youth, for clinging to him, but she shouted back at him and when the scene came to an end, she said she loved him no less.

When Ritter left London, Dikman returned from the Argentine, in flight from a mountain of unpaid bills and with a sense of failure. He was morose, uncivil; he spoke only of his misfortune. His arrival in London was untimely.

One of the players in the company he had abandoned had taken the lease of the only theatre devoted permanently to Yiddish plays. Dikman had to rent a hall and to give several performances under terrible conditions. Old friends came to see him, but the new playgoers had no taste for the old-fashioned plays Dikman put on. He aroused no curiosity. Nor could curiosity be stimulated by notices in the press, for publicity had to be adapted to British standards. Dikman had achieved a museum value. He could now be regarded as an item in a catalogue. He went through his old plays like an automaton. He played to get through with the performance. He was reduced to one pleasure. At his age, some take to drink, some to gambling, others to women. Dikman loved to eat.

He frequented a restaurant where Hungarian food was prepared. He often ate himself sick. Eating was one of the pleasures of the day that could be relied upon. His corpulence increased. His bulk was enormous. He moved about now with asthmatic convulsions that were terrifying. When he was taken sick, Dinah persuaded him to see physicians, but he never followed their advice. He quarreled with his wife only about food—when she had certain rich dishes removed from the table, or when she forced him to stick to his diet.

"Let's go back to New York," she said. She was tired and bored. The long overdue rent and salaries worried her, and she was anxious about the mood of her husband, which grew more and more disdainful of common sense.

"Until they ask me, I'll never go back," he shouted. He hated to think of another struggle. He hated to think of meeting Ritter again. He wanted to float along, eating and sleeping. He dreamed of a simple routine. He would be pleased to walk the same street to the theatre, visit the same restaurant every day, go to sleep in the same bed every night. He needed the protection of the old habits that could not easily be broken.

"You know—I'm thinking—maybe Odessa should be next," he said, his chin resting on his chest. "Come to think of it, it's really home. There would be old friends, old places, old restaurants—untouched by time."

So Dikman, his manuscripts, his old costumes—heavier than ever—and his wife returned to Odessa. He renewed old friendships, finding his friends older than he had pictured them. He visited old restaurants that were not as inviting as he had thought them in the days of his first exile. He made "touches" and it was not so easy. It was the old world, the old home, and more dilapidated than ever. The poor had become poorer; and while there were many who had become wealthier, they lived in a section far removed from the Jewish quarter.

Dikman gave Manewitz's "Kreutzer Sonata" as a new offering. By now it was an old play in New York, but this was his concession to the new currents in the theatre. He would show them that he could also play in the new plays.

All day long he was in a state of excitement. He ate a heavy meal at four; it was good. He wiped his lips complacently and patted his stomach. He spoke to Dinah and noting a look of anxiety in her eyes, said:

"I'll go back to the diet—I promise you—right after the first week. Don't worry!"

While he dressed, he felt short of breath. It was a touch of asthma. He sat in his chair, dozing, and aroused himself when he felt that he was falling asleep. He walked out of the warm dressing-room and stood in the wings. He asked whether Dinah was ready, and was assured that she was. He made his entrance to generous applause. He was playing the part of the father, who awaited the entrance of his daughter after having learned that she had been seduced by a Russian officer. He was to reprove her sharply, and to suggest an immediate marriage with an impecunious Jewish fiddler and their prompt departure for America. That was his part at that moment. He walked restlessly to and fro, watching the door through which Dinah, who played the daughter, was to enter. He was annoyed by the difficulty in breathing. He tried to loosen his collar, and felt better. There was a strange pain in his stomach, and he felt the blood rushing to his head. His eyes were covered with a film. The audience seemed to be swaying. He heard a faint shout, as if from the gallery. He thought of the time he had played in Odessa, when Goldfaden stood in the wings, cursing and urging him on to sing louder. He thought of his great performance in "Uriel Acosta," and how he had played Shylock. Now it was the old Windsor Theatre in New York, then the Pavilion in London, then the old barn in Buenos Aires. As Dinah came toward him through the door he made an effort to move and fell.

Dinah looked up in alarm. That was not in the part. She rushed toward him, and his staring eyes met hers in one long last gaze of reproach and affection, regret and fatigue. He was so tired. He tried to speak, but his tongue was not his to command. Others rushed on the stage. The curtain was lowered. A physician was summoned, but by the time he arrived Dikman was dead.

They said that Dikman was a fortunate man. His life ended where it began. Of how many Jews is that true? Their life begins in the East—their graves are far in the West. The fathers here, the children there. Dikman left home in Odessa and traveled all over the world, but he was buried in the Jewish cemetery near his own father in Odessa. There he rests in peace.

II

Mekler's Waterloo

IT IS SAID THAT GOD HUMBLES THE EXALTED AND RAISES THE humble. The wheel of life turns endlessly. That was what it was made for. Sometimes it moves as swiftly as though the lightning of God's wrath could not be held in check, and things tumble with a crash. The worm Man accumulates power, uninterruptedly, and feels secure, swelling with victory, unaware of the debacle that awaits him just around the corner.

Mekler was taken from the top seat and flung into the scrap-heap. There was no intermediate state.

He seemed immune. Nothing halted the progress of his fortunes. His world was just one theatre on the Bowery, and that he held in the palm of his hand. All that was in it was his property. All the puppets who played, the men who devised his plays, who manned the services of his theatre, were his slaves. He specialized in what were known as *shund* plays. He was the maker of melodramas. He used the stage to exploit sensational news stories. He dramatized the case

40

of the Italian murderess, Marie Barbiari. He gave the East Side the first story of Captain Dreyfus with musical interludes. He wrote a play on the famous poison case, the Molineux murder, finishing the last act while they were rehearsing the first. He staged burlesques, with bulging women in cotton tights, singing ragtime music. "Vulgarity here presented" should have been on the marquee of Mekler's theatre. Let others have the respect of the world; he was not seeking it. It was said that he had property in various forms, in many enterprises; that he had hidden away his profits here and there, so that none could guess the size of his fortune. But the hand of God smote him, and he fell. What he had was swept away in a night. His downfall was abrupt and complete.

When a man sees nothing ahead of him, he should prepare to retreat. A Waterloo may be avoided for a time. There it is, right ahead of you. As you move on, it comes nearer. But if you have sense, you throw sacrifices to the oncoming destroyer. All subsidiary interests should be discarded for the sake of progress, to get ahead. Abandon minor ambitions for the sake of the chief aim of your life, hoping that these sacrifices will postpone the day of reckoning. If you are unable to rid yourself of these petty ambitions or desires, if you really do not mean to concentrate upon "all or nothing," you will not meet a Waterloo; you will sink gradually into a morass and find yourself struggling for minor advantages; the end will be the same, but there will be no spectacular debacle.

Mekler fell from the top of a mountain. There he lay, every bone in his body crushed, every hope extinguished. That old man shuffling along, with rheumy eyes, one arm stiff, in dilapidated clothes, was all that was left. His descent was to the very bottom.

He came up from the slums of Odessa. He never knew of

home; he never knew of school; he never knew what it meant to have his hunger really satisfied. He remembered his youth as one long constant hunger. He prowled around the restaurants, inhaling the smells until he was given a job as an errand boy, then as a dishwasher, then as a waiter. When a Yiddish theatre was opened, he became an usher. When he grew up he haunted the brothels and served as a tout. He learned how to read, and the day he celebrated was the day when he was allowed to serve as a prompter. Then he stood up and ceased to be one of the unregistered. He came to New York with a group of hungry players who gave performances in a hall, where he served as bill-poster, usher, prompter, and eventually as writer of monologues. He had a natural talent for imitation and acquisition. He always took the things he could lay his hands on. Nothing not his own could exist in his presence. Where there were no leaders, he took the baton and led. Soon, having neither scruples nor good taste, he became the leader of his company. He had no liking for the make-believe of theatre, and could not impersonate vice or virtue, but he knew how to use both to serve his interest. He became the manager. He put together the plays. He chose the actors and made all business decisions. He had an eye for what would bring money into his pocket. He saw the value of the *shund* play. He knew that it appealed to the lawlessness of the new immigrants. He knew the value of the salacious jest, and how the suggestion of nakedness could lure people into the theatre. He pandered to his audiences, and his pandering brought money into his bank account. But he forgot to watch his step. A lust slumbered in his heart, waiting to be aroused, to take possession of him.

Mekler came to the theatre in a hurry and called for his

factotum Chayim. Of all the sycophants in his theatre, he
trusted only Chayim, who was a born lackey. At least Mekler thought so. Chayim seemed to like being ordered about
by a masterful man. Mekler liked to think that there was at
least one man in his theatre with whom he need not argue,
to whom orders could be given and were received without a
murmur, without comment, and carried out. He never saw
past the film that covered Chayim's eye, and never imagined
what he could be thinking of. Chayim behaved like an intelligent robot.

One of the scrubwomen hurried to bring Chayim while
Mekler paced the office. Chayim entered in a flutter and
saluted his chief, looking anxiously into his face to guess
what he wanted, anticipating the order he knew was about
to come. He behaved like a dog, scanning his master's features
for a sign. Mekler growled as he threw posters and programs
about the room, scolded Chayim for the disorder which he
himself was making, and finally said:

"I am going away for five days. Don't tell anybody I have
gone. You don't know where I am because I didn't tell you
—understand?"

Chayim was astounded. The boss was leaving the theatre
for five days. He never left the theatre. He was as regular
as the clock. You could tell in advance every move he would
make any day in the week. What was there to take him away
for five days at the height of the season, with benefits to be
arranged, repertoires to be fixed, and trouble brewing in
the company?

"Ox! Why do you stand looking at me like that?" exclaimed Mekler.

"Who is to be the boss while you are away?" asked Chayim, beside himself. "There are benefits—quarrels—bills to
be paid."

"Imagine you are the boss," said Mekler, looking over his cash-book, peering into his bank book, removing several checks. "All the money coming in, bank it. Pay no bills. If the women quarrel, tell them I'll settle their differences when I get back. But don't bother me, and don't try to find me. I'm gone—you hear?"

With that, he left by way of the alley.

Chayim just had to tell the news to Levin, the prompter, who, as was to be expected, passed it on to other interested parties. A feeling of relief spread through the theatre. Now they could draw a full breath. Now they could speak their minds. The evening's performance was remarkable for a certain jollity, a disregard of the prompter, and the improvising of dialogue, especially by the comedian. Now the angry eye of Mekler no longer restrained them. He was not watching them, cursing them under his breath. They played as though they were on holiday.

But he returned on Thursday, instead of Friday; they cursed their luck and resumed a submissive manner. He looked somewhat remorseful and called for a rehearsal, at which he poured out his wrath upon all the performers; nothing was being done as he wanted.

Mekler's vanishing act became a weekly event. He seemed worried. He no longer twirled his cane jauntily; he used it as a prop. A wrinkle of profound satisfaction hovered about his mouth, drawn with lassitude. Chayim was disturbed. He had his eyes glued to the account books, and seemed absorbed in his work; but every now and then he looked up at the ceiling, pondered, wondered what the world was coming to.

Schorr was not much of an actor, but he had his merits as a gossip. He had noticed the regular absences of Mekler and turned his nose to the sniffing of a scandal, for scandal there must be somewhere, as he knew from experience in the theatre. "When a creature like Mekler begins breaking the habits of a lifetime, there must be a scandal," he said. "A man doesn't break one set of habits without getting another."

He would have invented a tale at once, but he dared not take such liberties with his manager. He found ways to have Mekler followed on one of his weekly trips. The scent led out of the East Side, up to 61st Street. There he was seen entering an apartment house and emerging later with a woman on his arm.

Mekler's Waterloo was to be a woman—quite in harmony with the traditions of drama, quite in harmony with the biography of many a famous man in the theatre and in politics. Women have many uses—they serve for inspiration, for pleasure, for ornament, for social distinction; but in the world of business, where the conservation of energy is important, they are the worms that undermine the very foundations of life.

Mekler had never married. He was a bachelor by conviction and as a matter of expediency. He was busy conniving to make money. All his affairs of the heart were ordinary events in his life—like eating and smoking, drinking and gambling. He was a man of vigor and strong appetites; his affairs were average. But one thing you could be certain of: he never let them interfere with his business. He kept himself free from entanglements in the theatre, and even when one of his prima donnas made him break his rule, an affair with her usually meant that the next season she found herself kicked out of the company. But all his sex life had been lived in the purlieus of the Ghetto. It had never risen beyond 14th Street.

But he had reached the time of his life when sexual desire must produce new sensations or it becomes meaningless, and he had met one of those women who was an adept in the arts of "love." Her ancestry was Russian, and she had lived in Paris—where fornication has been refined to a degree that accounts for its renown as the center of the civilized world. She was vivacious, she was refined, she was a coquette; but all to the point of such refinement that only one experienced in the exercises she practiced could appreciate and resist. At first he thought that he would regain mastery over the situation after it had subsided to a normal beat.

But he had reckoned without the lady. She led him a costly dance, and when he felt that it was time to call a halt, he found himself enthralled, enchained to the desire. She was astonishing: she was cool and calculating even while seemingly in a fury of passion. She made him her slave. He could not take himself away. He lacked the strength to regain his freedom. So he gave up the struggle.

There she was, installed in a fashionable apartment furnished by a decorator. It was a warm, soft nest, into which he sank with a feeling of complete happiness. His vanity was fed. He was made to feel that he owned a woman who would be regarded as a credit to men of even greater wealth and reputation. But she had never been able to persuade him to display his conquest.

"You are ashamed of me," she said, reclining on a Turkish diven. He sensed that she must have taken a perfumed bath.

"Who could be ashamed of you, my dear?" he said. "But it would not do. The East Side would not understand. That is why we can't go over there."

"They might laugh at you," she murmured. "After all, why should an elderly, sedate man take up with a pretty young woman?"

Mekler looked at himself in the mirror. He was shocked. There were heavy bags under his eyes. He could not stand erect. His clothes did not fit. He was grieved that she should have made this unkind remark. His lower lip trembled.

"You have nothing to complain of," he said.

She laughed a loud, cynical laugh, with a challenging intonation. It alarmed Mekler; after all, there were limits. Lassitude crept over him.

But he did not go out with her to any of the noisy places she craved, nor did he ever take her to the East Side. He felt that he could not expose himself to public scrutiny; it would have been embarrassing; it required too much explanation and evasion. He made up for his refusal by lavish presents.

But her demands sent a chill down his spine. Dresses and jewelry, perfumes and laces. It was amazing how she could manage to strip him of whatever money he brought with him; and how she could worm promises out of him that had to be kept later. But still he thought she was worth it all.

His theatre moved into the red. There was no discipline, no order. Chayim seemed to have no head for business. All he knew was how to keep the books, and Mekler cursed him roundly, badgered him for the bills, glared into his eyes with murderous intent, but was restrained by what seemed to be innocence and loyalty. The income from benefits seemed to melt away; there were many extra charges; he could not believe his eyes when he saw the mounting figures of his own special account. Chayim told him of the intrigues of his company, but he brushed them off. Chayim shrugged his shoulders. Really, what was there to do? Why should he worry about a man who seemed intent upon doing away with himself? Every man to his own form of death, he decided.

Nor did Mekler foresee the collapse of that world he had segregated for his own exclusive use. The apartment he had furnished Thekla consisted of six large rooms. There were two servants who "lived in." Mekler was known as the uncle of their mistress. They were aware of the fiction, and were prepared to admit Mekler at any time. In spite of the tantalizing methods of his fair friend, he visited her as often as she permitted him to come. He marveled at her, she seemed so unwearied; he was determined not to let her feel his inferiority. He had vowed to stay away. Nevertheless, prompted by a desire to be refreshed by her vivacity, he came.

He was nervous and depressed. He knew that the theatre was the source of his trouble. There were difficulties in meeting his obligations. He had to offer some of his uptown properties for sale; this enabled him to go on. But the hectic color of his cheeks, the general debility from which he suffered, made him think that he was probably paying too much attention to Thekla. He should normalize his life. Business and pleasure should not be mixed. But he was like a drunkard or a drug addict. He had made this pleasure his master. In his sober moments, when his business sense ruled, he knew that she would ruin him. He felt that he was headed for a collision, but he had to go on.

He entered the apartment like a guilty school-boy. Wearily, he removed his overcoat, pushed back a few hairs from his forehead, and was about to enter Thekla's boudoir without ceremony when he heard a voice. It was not Thekla's.

He had been thinking, quite often, of the possibility of an end to his dream. She would tire of him, or take up with another man. That was why he gave in to her every whim and caprice. That would keep her indebted to him. He had taken for granted loyalty based upon self-interest.

The voice disturbed him. It was a man's voice. It was mingled with the soft murmur that came from Thekla. His heart contracted. He felt as if he had been struck an unexpected blow. His legs became weak and he was unable to move forward. He steadied himself as the conversation went on, and then entered the next room.

Thekla started from the divan in alarm, while the man who sat at her side rose carelessly. He was one of those young men who seem designed to impress with their masculinity. His self-assurance was reflected in the throw of his shoulders, the twirl of his moustache, his ease of manner. He was not disturbed by the entrance of Mekler. This was not an unusual scene for him. He was not frightened.

Thekla came forward with a smile and presented her new "cousin." When he heard the word, Mekler's face was distorted with anger. He felt a sense of outrage. Strangely, he seemed like a husband finding his privacy invaded.

"Liar," he said thickly. "No more your cousin than mine."

"Have it your way," she said. "Say he is my lover, then. Let me tell you, he's worth a hundred of you."

"After all I've done for you," he muttered. "Give and give. Takes the last drop of my blood, and that's not enough."

"It was worth all you gave me for me to stand you so long," she said brazenly, looking at the younger man.

Mekler saw naked depravity in the gleam of her eyes. They were passionate and could be filled with desire, but from behind the film, avarice and cruelty stared at you. There was no modesty in them; there was no reserve; physical passion was inseparable from calculation. He was horrified. But he shouted:

"All I had, I gave you. Have you no gratitude? I loved you, do you forget that? And that you loved me, do you

remember that? If you think he will give you more, why
don't you tell me how much?"

"You bore me," she said, gaining courage as she saw him
weakening. "And it isn't your money, either. I am tired of
being hidden away. I want to be free. It's time for you to
quit."

"To quit?" he echoed.

"That's it. I've had enough of you," she said finally, and
joined the young man, who stood at the window looking
out.

Mekler turned, as if looking for a seat, for something to
lean on, and stumbled. He regained his balance and tried
to speak, but had difficulty in finding his tongue. It had
become thick, hard to move. An agonizing pain shot through
him, and he felt himself lifted from the floor. A thousand
hammers beat in his head. All the blood rushed to his eyes.
His hands and feet shot out. He was doubled up on the
floor. Thekla turned and uttered a cry of horror. The young
man also rushed toward him. A knotted figure lay on the
floor, jerking about in convulsions.

"This looks bad," he said. "Let's get him to the couch."

He lay unconscious in the hospital for weeks. When he came
out he walked with a limp, and his mouth was twisted. He
mechanically wandered toward the theatre. The season was
over. The actors had left for the mountains. Chayim was in
charge. Mekler could not decipher the figures he showed
him. When he asked for the balance, Chayim went labo-
riously to the safe, produced a set of figures, and showed
them to him with a smile. It was all that was left of the
theatre. There was rent due, and the lease was gone. He
would have accused Chayim of duplicity, but he had no
strength for anger. The fact was, he could not speak dis-

tinctly. His legs were trembling under him. During the summer his body had recovered somewhat; he still had a few thousand dollars, but his occupation was gone.

Such was his perversity that, intent upon drinking to the dregs all that was left in the cup of life, he tried to see Thekla again. If she remained his friend, he might recover and find his place in the world round about him. He could begin over again, but he needed her physical presence. He wanted the physical touch of compassion.

She had no compassion. She was still living on the proceeds of the sale of the jewels he had given her, and while the money lasted, her companion was the debonair scoundrel whom Mekler had once seen. Mekler hovered about her apartment, eager to get a glimpse of her, but she was relentless.

One day, she sent her maid out to invite him up, and told him the frank truth: he was obnoxious to her. She did not want him to haunt her. She had a new fish on her hook, and he was timid. Mekler was spoiling the affair. As a favor, he should go away and not trouble her any more.

He said he would die if she cast him off. She told him to go away and do that. He said he had a few thousand dollars left; he would give them to her. For a moment she looked at him. His hair was white, his mouth drooped, his body was a bag of bones, and he leaned on a cane. He was not a pleasant object. She made a gesture as if wishing to erase the picture. He stumbled away and did not come again.

Soon, all desire and ambition died in him. He lost interest in money, in business, in food. He suffered another stroke and was laid up for several months. Again, he gradually recovered. He suffered no pain. He was numb in body, incoherent in speech, bewildered in thought. He lived in a hall bedroom on 4th Street, alone. His theatre was now taken over by Ritter. A new class of plays was being given. *Shund* was driven into the music halls. Within a year after his debacle, Mekler was forgotten.

He shuffles into one of the cheaper coffee-houses and seats himself at a table with difficulty, and orders tea. He seems absorbed in his own thoughts. He looks neither to the right nor to the left. Objects pass him unnoticed. The older actors pass him on the street, barely recognizing him; when they do, they wonder what has come over him. They see that he is partly paralyzed in arm and leg, but what about his fortune invested uptown, downtown, everywhere? What has struck him? He often forgets to pay for his tea.

One evening, as they saw Mekler passing, Schorr, who talks in the style of classic melodrama, made an attempt to deliver the judgment of posterity. He said:

"Mekler climbed a pyramid and stood on its apex. He was domineering and proud. He was heartless. He never looked around. He had his eyes glued on the goal. He wanted to make money, lots of it. He was too absorbed in climbing, and developed just one vice. That was a worm gnawing at entrails for a long time. When he reached the very top and felt himself secure, suddenly, without warning, with no hint of disaster, it toppled over and buried him. He is the living remnant of the wreck. The wonder is that so much of him is still alive."

III

The Moth

THE YIDDISH THEATRE LAY IN A CORNER OF THE GHETTO, beckoning the aliens to enter a world of play, and in a niche of that corner, where that world did not enter, an atom of Jewish humanity had attached itself; it was known as Yekl. While the outer world was busied with sweatshops, politics, art, ambitions, and controversy, he was dedicated to serve as a mender of the garments of the players.

Yekl was one of the great Ritter's costumers. The dressing-room of ths Yiddish actor was the center and circle of his life. A new play meant nothing more to Yekl than a new robe, the refurbishing of an old pair of sandals, or the trimming of an old coat. He knew the play by the costume Ritter wore, and to him it had as many acts as there were changes.

He took his noonday meal in an actors' coffee-house, about two hundred feet from the theatre. His bosom friend was the hairdresser, known as Zhulik, a tall, lanky, nonchalant fellow with whom he had one thing in common. Both would berate Ritter for his miserliness—Yekl in the matter of costumes, Zhulik in the matter of cosmetics, wigs, perfumes, etc.

One day, at lunch, Zhulik raised his big eyes and said:

"Tomorrow, Yekl, he plays Uriel Acosta. But what can I do? The same old wig, and not a cent for anything to make him presentable."

"He wears out a mantle in two months," said Yekl, "and when I talk to him of a new mantle, a new hat, he tells me people don't come to see his clothes."

At home—that is, the place around the corner where he slept and ate his suppers—Yekl punctuated his hurried meals with cryptic allusions to surprises he had in store for theatregoers when Ritter appeared in his new play. Asked what the play was about, what kind of part the great actor would enact, he would declare:

"He will be a Spanish grandee in a black mantle this time, but what a cloak I have made over for him!"

He had served Ritter for fifteen years, entering his services upon his arrival in New York. Friends said to him:

"Well, Yekl, how long, how long?"

"What do you mean, how long?" he replied. "When I was a tailor, at home, I made coats, but who wore them? Anybody, everybody, I never really knew. Now I make a suit for a Spanish grandee, I decorate cardinals, kings, generals, grand inquisitors, high priests, and Herr Ritter is my model; that's work for you!"

Yekl almost never visited other theatres; that is, he seldom saw a play with the audience. He was too busy. When he visited Burlak's theatre he repaired at once to the dressingroom, three flights above the stage, and heard only the shouts, screams, shuffling, snatches of music, and cheers; he was interested in the work of his colleague, the costumer there.

In fact, Yekl had never left the East Side Ghetto. He was tied, as it were, within a circle four hundred feet in diameter, whose limits were his lodgings and Ritter's theatre. In the summer, when the actors left for the mountains, he acted as the watcher and spent his time puttering over the costumes. On the eve of the Day of Atonement, when no performances were given, he would almost die for lack of employment. Broadway was an unknown continent, Harlem a far-off city, and the Bronx another province. He saw Brooklyn Bridge dimly from a distance, and remembered Castle Garden only to wonder where in the world it was; he believed it to be south of the theatre, but had never gone to see. He did not read the Yiddish papers, except the headlines of reviews of plays, and though he was the son of orthodox parents he never went into a synagogue, except once to hear the leader of Ritter's chorus chant the services.

"I saw a play on Broadway last night," said Zhulik to him one day. "It was wonderful."

"Wonderful costumes, I suppose," asked Yekl.

"The scenery was the finest I ever saw," said Zhulik.

"Don't we have sceneries, too?" remarked Yekl. "What is the good of sceneries in a play? What do people go to the theatre for? What is a play? People! And it is not the people, but the costumes they wear, that brings the crowd."

"I can get a pass for you to see it," ventured Zhulik.

"Who wants to see such trash?" retorted Yekl.

"You are getting run down, Yekl," said Zhulik. "You ought to take the boat to Coney Island. Treat yourself to a change of scenery."

"I get seasick," said Yekl.

"Take the car," suggested Zhulik.

"Then where is the pleasure?" asked Yekl.

"Don't you ever want to go out and get some fresh air?" exclaimed Zhulik, exasperated. "Sixteen years in this country and never seen Coney Island or the Bronx! Don't you like to travel?"

"Why should I go to the Bronx? You ride I don't know how long, and what do you see? I have never heard tell what they see what makes it worth going to," he said.

"Why, the trees and the flowers and the menagerie," explained Zhulik.

"Animals don't interest me," said Yekl.

"I've a good idea," said Zhulik, when the season was drawing to its close. The weather was cool; a fresh breeze was blowing. "Let us go to Brooklyn. We'll see how Tobias is getting along with his theatre in Brownsville."

For Zhulik was disturbed by Yekl's sallow cheeks and noticed that he had acquired a cough.

"Let me be, Zhulik," he said. "The East Side here is good enough for me. I can't understand why people, like birds, should always be on the move. There isn't a tenement on Forsythe Street, near the theatre, where I haven't lived. And I've lived on Chrystie Street and on Hester. I've moved enough in my time."

He concluded his apology with a fit of coughing.

As Ritter was leaving for the summer he looked Yekl over curiously and frowned. He asked:

"Yekl, maybe you, too, should go away for the summer? Maybe the mountains?"

"Where should I go in the mountains, Herr Ritter? I watch the theatre and fix up your old costumes. And believe me, if you once spent a few dollars for new costumes it wouldn't do you the least bit of harm."

"Ah, *soi?*" murmured Ritter, stroking his chin where the stage beards were wont to hang. "Don't you worry about my new costumes! You are going to take a vacation this summer, and that's all! You come to this country and see nothing of the great America discovered by Columbus. You sit here in the dark theatre and cough your lungs away. And if you should die, whom will the union blame for it? Ritter, you can bet. You'll go to the Catskills, you hear, and drink milk and eat raw eggs and get some fresh air, that's all. You hear?"

Yekl heard, and was silent. The thought of raw eggs nauseated him. He wondered what was wrong with the air on the East Side. He shrugged his shoulders after Ritter had departed and turned to his work.

Ritter enjoyed a vacation of four weeks. He returned to his own world with an unmistakable tan and a trifle more weight. He was rounded out snugly. He had tasted the pleasures of the mountain, sat on the porch in a sport shirt, zealously played poker in the open air; and he was refreshed.

Yekl raised his head and greeted his employer with a wan smile.

"How-de-do, Herr Ritter," he murmured.

"Still here, the imbecile!" said Ritter as he passed into his office. Yekl's cheeks were sunken, his shoulders bent, his eyes watery, and his mouth seemed wider than before. When Ritter returned there was a menace in the look he threw at Yekl.

"It is enough, Yekl, it is enough! What do you think? Do I want a funeral in my theatre? Look at your face how it looks, your clothes hang like bags on you. You want to play hide and seek with the Angel of Death, eh? Not if I know it! Here is one hundred dollars; with this you go to the moun-

58 Tales of the Yiddish Rialto

tains and stay there for seven weeks, and if I see you before that, you're sacked! Positively!"

He gave Yekl no opening for a discussion. He ordered Zhulik to pack Yekl's trunk, purchase his ticket, give him a timetable, and the address of a boardinghouse in the Catskills, and said good-bye. When he saw Yekl's eyes fill with tears, he said:

"Yekl, don't be a fool! To live in this world you must take care of your lungs. Don't I know the mountains are no good? But doctors say different. Be a good fellow, come back good and strong, and I'll raise your wages right away."

Zhulik went with the bewildered Yekl to the station and when he shook hands for the last time told him to drink cod-liver oil.

"All he needs is fresh air," murmured Zhulik to himself.

But the health-giving air of the mountains, the aroma of the pine woods, the nourishment of raw eggs, fresh milk, and complete rest were not destined for Yekl. Two days later Chayim, the cashier, peeping through the circular hole at the window, saw Yekl gazing at him. His face had a look of terror on it. He blinked his eyes, gasped for breath and held a handkerchief to his mouth. He saluted Chayim with a nod. Chayim emerged from the box office.

"Now you'll catch it when Ritter sees you!"

"What can I do, dear Chayim? I won't go back there for no amount of money. It's cold up there, no fire can warm you. All day and night the wind blows, and open windows they won't let me shut; and at night, open windows. Why does he bother me? The air in New York is a hundred times better than there. What do I get from it? Look at this!"

And he showed Chayim his handkerchief covered with blood, and when he coughed one heard a rasping in his throat.

The eminent tragedian was seated in the foyer of his theatre, fanning himself, although it was quite cool, when Yekl presented himself and stood before him with such abject humility and wretchedness depicted on his face that he was forced to say, softly:

"Well, what do you want, *podletz*?"

Yekl gave him, as reply, a roll of bills and said:

"Here is seventy dollars, what I got left. I owe you thirty, and you can take it off my wages."

"What wages?" exclaimed Ritter in a rage. "Whose wages? Did any one ask you about wages? I send him away he should get well; he talks to me of wages! What can I do with you, Yekl? What is there to do with you? I ask you, can you fix my costumes when you spit your lungs out with blood? What will people say of me now, that you got consumption working for me? I'll have to see a doctor with you right away."

Yekl followed him meekly to the office of Dr. Kamenetz, who stripped him, examined him, and then took Ritter aside and spoke to him in a low tone of voice.

"The doctor says, Yekl," said Ritter, "you must get on a diet. What is a diet? You must eat things good for you; you must sleep with open windows, and you must be all day in the open air. Now, you don't want to go to the mountains, so you must sleep in the Bronx. And to have you do something, I'll get you a stand in front of the theatre, and every night for three hours you sell candies, fruits, and make your living. If you want to go to the mountains I pay your expenses; if not, you must do it yourself. Suit yourself."

For weeks Yekl walked about as in a dream. He was meditating what to do. His experience in the mountains had been terrifying. One did not feel people around one; Nature, bleak and uncouth, subject to fierce outbreaks of temper, encompassed one. Life was an endless soliloquy. Yet there was health and physical life. And to leave the theatre and peddle fruit in the lobby, and to miss that intimate touch with the dressing-room, the exhilaration which had been his when he brought Ritter a newly patched garment to wear; not to see the machinery that made out of the great Ritter, whose voice could roar like a bull or whimper like a child, one night the great Uriel Acosta, the next night the sad, mystical "Black Jew," who forsook his parents for Christianity; one night the distressed father, the next Hamlet; one night to see the patriarchal elders of the ancient city of Jerusalem, the next the pomp and glory of the Jews in Spain—not to see all this magnificence in such costumes!

At least to be within hearing of the theatre, where he could listen to the comments of the audience between the acts, where he could meet Zhulik and converse with him on the affairs of their world, was to be preferred to the solitude of the mountains. The mountains, Yekl might have said, if he had been gifted with speech, were too close to God, and he was afraid. He did not dare look at God when He frowned.

He moved up to the Bronx, and a few weeks later he came to Ritter and said:

"Herr Ritter, give me what to peddle and I'll peddle."

The actor laid his hand upon Yekl's matted hair and said with feeling:

"Yekl, believe me, if you had done what I told you, you wouldn't be what you are now. But there is no use talking with you, *podletz*; you want to stay with me and die. All right. Do you think I was going to leave you peddle and maybe not make a good living, and starve instead of getting well? I want you to live, Yekl! You belong to me, and the union and the whole world can say what they please of me —you'll take care of yourself until you're well."

But Yekl preferred to hang around the lobby in the
evenings, with some visible reason for doing so. He pro-
cured his basket, with which he came downtown every
evening and sold his wares to the audience that saw Ritter
play. He coughed and spat, but he could not tear himself
away. He was a moth fascinated by the flame. He was like
an iron filing drawn to the magnet. He had to stick there
even if he died. And so he coughed, and breathed in the
foul air of the lobby of the theatre, and while he lived
felt happy.

The actors whom he saw leaving the theatre after the
performances would say in whispers:

"On the stage we give plays, and he coughs his life away."

The great Wonder-Worker whose minions had given the
Children of Israel the world of play, once relaxing from
matters of graver import, asked His angels abruptly how
His child Isroelik was taking to the toy they had provided
him with, and they answered:

"It seems to amuse him, and then he quarrels about it;
and curses; but in the long run it seems to amuse him."

Had they seen Yekl one night as he dragged himself home-
ward, with a handkerchief to his mouth, convulsed by a fit
of coughing, they would not have given that report. There
was no amusement in that tragedy.

IV

Badchen in Pastel

IT SELDOM HAPPENS TO A MAN THAT HE CAN LOOK BACK AT his life and see himself in perspective as though he had once lived and died and been reincarnated into a new body. That was what happened to Lazar Badchen. When he lost his voice, the comedian ceased to live, and for two years while he struggled to be reborn he was dead to the stage. He was isolated from life by a veil of uncertainty. He heard the sounds that rose from the noisy city. He saw people moving near and far. He heard the rattling of the elevated trains, the rumbling of the streetcars, the hum of conversation. But he was mute. In that period of silence he was reborn.

The Badchen of that period was a comedian of comedians. He was as agile as an antelope. His gestures, his grimaces, his jests, clever and vulgar—in all these he had no rival. He could play without rehearsal, depending upon the prompter, snatching the words off his lips instantaneously, with intel-

ligence. There were parts made for him. There were songs
he made famous. There was a Badchen walk, a Badchen
joke, a Badchen song. He never had a voice, but he knew
how to sing a patter song, delivering it with his hands and
feet. It was a good talking voice, rasping, somewhat hoarse,
but he made it serve all his needs.

His voice began to leave him. He had frequent colds.
The gallery boys now shouted, "Speak up, Badchen!" The
manager was alarmed. "Haven't you noticed it?" he asked
Badchen. "What?" said Badchen. "Your voice, *yold*," said
the manager.

Badchen was alarmed. He spoke to his wife. Libby was
a shrewd, sensible woman who was proud of the care she
gave the volatile genius. She suggested that he see a doctor
right away. There was no reason to be alarmed, but it was
always good to talk to a doctor.

So he saw a "professor." The professor looked down his
throat, looked into his ears, shoved him around a bit, advised him not to smoke, not to use stimulants, and not
to get himself excited. He gave him a bottle of medicine.

In order to reassure himself, Badchen stationed a friend
in the gallery. His voice came up there in a faint whisper.
A few nights later he repeated the experiment from the
second balcony. There he could not be heard at all. Within
a fortnight his voice dwindled to a whisper and the orchestra
seats could not hear him.

"Well, Libby, what do you say?" he whispered to his wife.

"Thank God, we have a little money saved," she replied
cheerfully. "You will go to the leading throat specialists and
they will cure you. Voices aren't lost like pennies. It'll
come back to you in time. Why shouldn't your voice take a
vacation? You've been using it for twenty-five years, making
it play all sorts of pranks. It is now taking a vacation without leave."

He suffered torments during the few weeks after he first knew his voice was leaving him. Men in ordinary pursuits of life are not so seriously crippled when their voices give them difficulty. A lawyer has a cold; his larynx gets out of order; he gets along without it. But the voice of an actor is his principal stock in trade. He ceases to live the moment his voice leaves him. His whole life depends upon being heard. Badchen felt that his life was oozing away with his voice.

But there was no postponing the inevitable. One night, playing his old part in "Schmendrik," he found that his lips were dry and no sound came from his throat. He stood before the large audience totally dumb. He looked over the footlights with terrified eyes. The curtain had to be lowered and the audience dismissed.

Badchen looked at his friends, who had gathered about him, with the eyes of a man not exactly certain whether he was about to die or whether it had not already happened. They shook hands with him as though saying goodbye forever. They felt that he was passing out of their world. He was cut off from the stage. He would never see the footlights again. He would never hear their applause again.

The physicians prescribed that he take a rest, that he gargle some awful medicine. His throat was burned by every physician he visited. They took his ten-dollar bills in a depressed sort of way as though they knew they were doing him no good. The money was "thrown away." Finally, he himself was convinced that all his sacrifices were leading him nowhere. So he passed out of the Yiddish Rialto.

One evening, months later, he was seated on a bench on Riverside Drive, looking at the New Jersey shore with melancholy eyes. It was his favorite pastime to go uptown in the evening and take the air near Grant's Tomb. Not even his wife's company was endurable. With the glimpse he received into the greater mysteries of life while gazing at the placid Hudson and at the twinkling lights across the river and on the passing steamers, he could think of himself without intrusion. He was muffled in a heavy fur coat and sat with his hands deep in his pockets. His attention was attracted by a man sitting on the same bench, who seemed interested in the lights. Every now and then, the man raised both arms high in the air, breathed deeply and stretched his long frame with evident enjoyment.

"There is nothing to make one feel calmer than a scene like this," he said to Badchen. "The great trouble with the world," he continued, paying no attention to Badchen's silence, "is the loss of faith. It is a scene like this, with sombre nature lying before one, and all the puny differences of mankind hidden under the mantle of night, that enables one to realize God's truth, that all is well in this world when thoughts are healthy and hopeful."

Badchen shook himself out of his reverie.

"But where can one get the strength to hope?" he whispered.

The stranger saw that Badchen was in trouble. "Let us walk," he said. They walked in silence while he talked on. They left the Drive and entered 125th Street; the stranger invited Badchen into a coffee-house and they sat down. The man ordered a glass of hot milk.

"You will have the same," he said.

After the milk was served, the stranger said:

"What is the trouble?"

Badchen explained in a whisper.

"Have you seen a physician?" asked the stranger. Badchen

nodded. "And they can do nothing for you? That's good. You are just the man I want to see," said the stranger finally, taking a card from his pocket. "You will come to see me tomorrow and I shall take care of you. God has given me power and I shall give His Power to you."

Badchen looked at the card. The man was a health adviser. His name was Dacosta.

Badchen came to Dacosta's house the next morning in an excited mood. The conversation had impressed him. There had been such absolute certainty in Dacosta's tones that Badchen felt certain he had a secret remedy. At the same time, what he said seemed so sensible, so clearly in accord with his own feelings, that he was determined at least to hear him further. He was ushered into a parlor and told to sit down. The room was comfortably arranged. The paintings on the wall were all outdoor scenes. The room was filled with soft chairs, a lounge, a bookcase, and in the rear he could see a library that looked so cozy that he was tempted to enter it. Just then Dacosta came in.

Badchen now had an opportunity to see him better. He was a dark, old man. His face was furrowed with wrinkles. But these wrinkles did not give him an austere or aged appearance. They made his face seem all the more genial, glowing, and trustworthy. His beard was gray and his hands were long and tapering. He wore slippers and a long dressing-gown of subdued coloring.

"I had thought of your comfort," he said as he shook Badchen's hand warmly, "and was about to ask you to step in here."

Badchen seated himself and let his frame relax.

"You may not know it," said Dacosta," but I am a physician and I know the secrets and techniques of medicine. I know the ancient drugs and all the modern concoctions."

Badchen looked about and saw no instruments, no oper-
ating chair, no X-ray machine, such as he had seen in other
physicians' offices.

"But the medicine I now use is Faith," Dacosta said, and
seated himself facing Badchen.

"Let me tell you, my friend," he continued. "You are
suffering from an impediment of speech and you think that
medicines can help you, but you can take all the medicines
all the quacks of the world may give you and none of them
will do you any good. Everything depends upon what you
have in you. If you have not got that quality in you, the
medicine is like water. You have lost courage. You are
despondent. You are willing to give up. You have no faith.
But once rid yourself of your despondency, regain your
faith, determine not to give up and you will be liberated
from the error of your ways."

Badchen felt himself enveloped in a warm, cordial, reassuring atmosphere and sank back into his chair with a feeling of great comfort.

"God has given you a body, but you were to be the
master of that body. Your mind was to rule it. You were not
to allow it to become the usurper of your spirit," Dacosta
said. "How do you expect to live if there is no will to live?
All the ills of the body are due to a refusal to assert oneself.
All you need do is cling more firmly to God and your
strength will return. From Him you will get all your
strength."

Badchen had not been a believer in anything. The God
of Israel had never spoken to him. He had never heard His
voice. His soul was empty. He had lived a frivolous life. He
had been thoughtless, self-centered. It felt very pleasant to
know that God was interested in his poor weak body, and
that with God's spirit he could overcome his infirmity. He

smiled at the man who had brought him this comfort and listened with sensual pleasure as Dacosta went on talking in his soft, rhythmic voice: his voice became sterner, more commanding.

"You think you are suffering from an impediment of speech. You think you cannot use your voice," he said "but you have got that all wrong. There is nothing the matter with your speech. You are just as well as anybody else. But you will not recover your voice until you have the faith to use it."

Badchen looked intently at the man before him. He saw in his eyes the light of firm confidence, of resoluteness, and he felt that he could trust him.

"Into your hands I place myself absolutely," he whispered.

"Absolutely?" Dacosta inquired.

"Yes," Badchen murmured.

"Very well, then," said Dacosta. "You will follow my directions precisely. You could use your voice in four weeks, but I shall not permit you to do so for six months to come. In the meantime, you must not utter, from the moment you leave this house, one syllable to anyone. I forbid you to speak. Communicate with your family by the written word or signs. You will rest, you will meditate, you will gather all your strength together, and in six months you shall use your voice again. And it will be your old voice, but purified, stronger, and you will think of the good you will do humanity by your humor, your good cheer, and you will be again what you were before you lost faith and hope. Do you agree?"

"Absolutely," murmured Badchen, extending his hand. Dacosta took his hand, shook it heartily and then ordered a glass of milk brought in, which Badchen drank with zest.

"Come to me every month and tell me how you are getting on. I shall keep in touch with you. My prayers will reach you," he said to Badchen as he was leaving.

When Badchen returned home his wife greeted him with a word of good cheer. He did not reply, but went to his desk, drew forth a pad, and wrote down his experiences with the healer. She read it and patted him on the back, but said:

"But how do you know he's not a faker?"

"Trust him," Badchen wrote. "With faith I can be healed."

In order to avoid inquiries he stored his furniture, leased a cottage in a New Jersey winter resort for six months, told under fifty, having no children of his own, he had not given his wife to let it be known that her husband could not speak, and left New York.

Badchen spent his time in the contemplation of nature. He read books of poetry and history, and soaked up the contents of small volumes sent to him by Dacosta.

His wife became impatient.

"I'm dying to hear your voice, Lazar," she said. "I'm sure if you tried you could speak now."

"It is not a question of speaking now," Badchen wrote on his pad. "It is a question of having faith. Until the inner strength returns, I shall not use my voice. Until the Master permits it, I shall not speak one word."

For he was thinking of many things he had side-stepped during his life. He had never thought of his relation to God or to the world. He had avoided such subjects, and being a thought to the problems of life. Now he was interested in the ultimate end of existence, and though his mind was unused to intellectual exercise, he soon acquired some notion of his place in the world.

He wandered about the seashore and saw the sun rise, and then in the evening, after it had warmed the earth, he saw it sink in the west. He felt himself to be a mere atom, but then remembered that he had in himself the spirit of God and took courage and pride in the fact that he could become master of himself. And he vowed that when he returned to his profession he would use what God had given him with more respect than ever before.

Three weeks before his period of probation was over Badchen returned to New York with his wife. He furnished his flat and went to see Burlak. When he entered the theatre the hangers-on, the loitering players, the ushers, all looked up with amazement depicted on their faces.

"See now, he's come back," they whispered, but none of them had the courage to come forward to greet him. He smiled and passed in to see Burlak. He handed him a piece of paper as soon as he entered. The manager read it, looked at Badchen, and shook his head.

"I will have to converse with you in writing," read the slip of paper. "I come to tell you that in three weeks I shall be able to use my voice. I am prepared to act. Select the play, announce my return, and we shall continue our contract of a year ago. I shall not open my mouth to speak until I appear on the stage."

"How do I know that you will even then be able to speak?" asked Burlak skeptically. "I'm sure I would like to have you back, but I must be certain that when I make the announcement you will be able to make good."

"You have my word for it," wrote Badchen on his pad. "If I do not make good I am willing to forfeit every cent I have left in the world."

"I'll have to consult my partner," said Burlak. "You wait one minute and I'll see Schnutzer."

Burlak returned in five minutes.

"Schnutzer is a good businessman," he said, "and he thinks we could venture it on one condition. You must play in a serious play."

"Agreed. I'm willing to play in Manewitz's new play," he wrote on his pad.

The announcement that Badchen was to return to the stage was greeted with tumultous joy, although in the coffee-houses the skeptics, who thought the world waited on their decision, were certain that Burlak would play a trick on his audience. But the people who remembered Badchen, who had felt a personal loss in his misfortune, rejoiced. The newspapers spoke of the matter with some suspicion as to the actual return of Badchen's voice and hinted that no-body, after all, had yet heard him speak.

Badchen kept himself in retirement. He did not venture into the coffee-houses. He spent his time in his room. He himself had no doubt of the outcome. He felt within him-self such contentment, such resolution, such good health, that he was certain that his voice too must have shared in the general good health of his body. His wife, however, trembled at the thought of failure. She hid all doubts from him. She expressed such cheerful certainty that her husband was deceived.

The theatre was packed to the doors that night. The gal-lery had a tumultous audience. The boxes were filled, the orchestra was compelled to play from the wings. There was intense interest; the atmosphere was suffocating to the tensely waiting audience.

The curtain went up. On the stage were seated three characters, with Badchen in the center as the old father helping his grandniece pluck feathers from geese. First the women talked with animation, and then it was Badchen's turn to speak.

It seemed an eternity while the audience waited. The players in the wings of the stage, Burlak in a box, all waited for Badchen to utter the first word. It was as though the play had stopped, or as though an intermission had been announced. It was so quiet that the prompter's voice, giving Badchen the first few words of his part, could be heard even in the gallery. The whole theatre seemed to be holding its breath.

Then Badchen spoke. The speech was a mere two sentences, a humorous sally at the expense of the young woman seated near him, but it rang out clearly, like a bell, and rose and penetrated the gallery and came back again. Badchen could speak!

A low, scarcely audible cheer broke from the audience, and soon swelled in volume until it shook the house. The audience rose, cheering, laughing, shouting "Come forward, Badchen; come forward" and a huge bouquet of flowers was shoved on the stage by an usher. Badchen came forward to receive it, but still they shouted, crying, "Speech, Badchen? speech!"

He saw before him a sea of happy, demonstrative faces; he felt overpowered by this ocean of good feeling. He wished to speak again, but could not find his voice. He burst into a fit of hysterical crying and fell into the arms of his fellow players. The curtain was rung down.

The disorder in front of the curtain was indescribable. There were many who believed that the actor had lost his voice again. A number said that it was not really Badchen

but a player who had been made up to look like him. There
were curses, tears were shed, and a number were in favor
of whipping Burlak at once.

Then the curtain went up slowly. Badchen was before
them again. He continued his playing as if nothing had
occurred to disturb his career. He played his part that night
superbly.

This was Badchen's second birth. He emerged fresh and
clean. He felt as though God had given him not only a new
body and a new voice but a new soul. He rid himself of his
zest for buffoonery. He felt nauseated when he heard the
prompter whispering an off-color joke, and refused to pick
it up. Why distort the flimsy types he was called upon to
play, why exaggerate their frailties, when the truth could
endow them with deeper colors? Why add to the natural
disfigurements of human beings by mocking them? He felt
overpowering sympathy for all human weaknesses, for the
suffering of the deformed, for the tragedy of life itself. He
could not bear to look at the comic masks of the old parts
he had played—the red-beards, the hunchbacks, the deformed
noses, the stammerers and stutterers. He laid away the be-
draggled figures in the storage room of the theatre. He destroyed the photographs he had accumulated and tried to
forget the world out of which he had emerged.

And this was the miracle. In two years of his second life
Badchen created the gallery of Jewish characters that distinguished his talent and genius. There were no *schmend-
ricks*. There were no dancing jesters. There were no red-
haired villains. There were no off-color jokes. The stuttering
Kunelemel disappeared.

Badchen was the rabbi in "God of Vengeance." He was
the old man in Manewitz's "God, Man and Devil." He was

the rabbi in "Uriel Acosta." Who will ever forget the old man in "Die Schechita," fluttering about his daughter whom he had forced into a tragic marriage? He was Lukas in Gorky's "Nachtasyl." In every great play of the period Badchen occupied a distinguished place. He was no longer a singer or dancer or buffoon. He was not a *letz* or *comediant*. He was an actor—an eminent member of a great profession.

His wife died young; he was left alone. It was unbearable to live without her. When the time came for him to make his final exit, it was not because of his heart or blood pressure or any hardening of the arteries. His voice went first. It seemed that Faith had merely arrested the cancer in his throat to enable him to make his life worthy of his great talent. Faith could hold out no longer, and the disease killed him after a few months of cruel pain.

V

Manewitz Arrives

IF YOU ASKED GOLDFADEN WHAT HE HAD IN MIND WHEN HE wrote his first operetta, he would have been at a loss to explain. "The old Jewish ailment, *parnosseh*." He had a living to make. Historians, however, would not accept this suggestion. They would say that his ambition was to create a theatre for his people, that he had it in mind to make a contribution to the culture of his people. That was why he cast the Yiddish theatre in the mold of the Purim carnival, and peopled the stage with strange figures called back to life from legend and Biblical story. He got his music from the old synagogue chants, the Chanukah and Purim melodies and the *opéra comique* of Paris, echoes of which had reached Rumania and Russia.

After Goldfaden, his imitators built upon the foundation he had laid, but broadened the horizon and cheapened the world. They made a hash of sacred and profane—of things Jewish and things alien. In their plays the comic and tragic

locked arms and went into a grotesque dance. They thought
their first concern was to make the audience laugh and cry
alternately. There was no middle ground. They were extravagant in language and in action. They disregarded tradition and improvised legend. They stole plots and distorted
them. Their profanity penetrated down to all the vulgarities
latent in Jewish life. What they wrote was called *shund*—
trash.

Then came Manewitz.

There is nothing more embarrassing to genius than to be
discovered by mediocrity, which then becomes its chronicler
and interpreter. Samuel Johnson must have despised Bos-
well. The little runt was always tagging at his heels, nailing
the wisecrack at white heat, and distorting it through eager
ineptitude. You could always count upon that scoundrel
being present, taking notes, never mislaying them—a pest
and a nuisance. The discoverer gets the habit of haunting
the scene, lingering after he has outlived his usefulness. He
is an ancestor you cannot get rid of. He has you down in
his notebook—what you ate, how you slept, what you
said. He will not let genius have its privacy, not if he can
help it. He is the ever-present interlocutor playing, as he
thinks, the more important part. Genius never is able to
see itself. It is the discoverer who knows it in all its changes,
all its moods. At the birth of the phoenix he was the mid-
wife; and he will not let the world forget it, and least of
all the phoenix himself.

It was Fusher who discovered Manewitz and wrote his
biography. His nose was made for intrusion. He had a bald
head even as a youth, long legs that got entangled under
tables and in chairs, an Adam's apple that danced about
nervously, like a ship in a storm. It was he who dragged
Manewitz out of the obscurity of journalism into the glare
of the footlights.

In those days every writer had a cause. It was indispensable, no less than pen and paper. The cause identified the writer. (In Manewitz's day it was said that the writer had to have a *Weltanschauung*. Nowadays they call it ideology.) It was the cause which poisoned the writer's pen and made him a propagandist. Art for art's sake was an abomination, an escape for the frustrated middle class. You had to have something to get angry about if you wanted to be a writer. But every professional writer had a sideline. They were leaders, advertizing agents, news dealers, ticket sellers, cigarmakers, teachers, bookkeepers or peddlers. They took revenge for their economic slavery and their humiliation in the things they wrote. They wanted to destroy the Old World. They were kept alive by their hatreds and prejudices, and they looked down upon the man who had no ideal as a middle-class reactionary.

Manewitz had no ideals that could be identified in the American scene. It was said that in Russia he was a disciple of the Tolstoyan simple life. He wanted Jews to go back to the land, and was against Talmudical dialectics. But the glamor of all ideas had been washed away in crossing the Atlantic. On the East Side he was merely a writer. He wrote Russian by preference, and Yiddish because he had to. Give him paper and pencil and an ample supply of cigarettes, and he would scribble for hours. No burning cause ever seared him. At times he was a socialist, but he was never unduly excited on the subject. He could not whip himself into an enthusiasm. He would rebuke the talkers at his table with the advice, "Don't excite yourself." He liked hearty laughter, hated obscenity, despised card-playing, and spent many hours at the chessboard. He wrote anything that came to mind, in any form that struck his fancy—sketches, book reviews, essays, novels. He sent his best manuscripts to Russia. He also gave "lessons." He looked like a grand duke,

built on a large scale, with huge appetites which were hard
to satisfy. But he was seldom far from starvation. He would
not talk of himself or his privations. Not that he was humble.
On the contrary, he was one of the rudest and most arrogant
of all the intellectuals. He would walk from East Broadway
to Brooklyn, lacking the fare, and never speak of it. He
disdained to mention the trivial. He had a wife and a large
brood of children. She was a buxom woman, somewhat dull,
and she would mutter behind his back, despairing of ever
having him think of domestic affairs. She was sensible enough
to avoid argument with him.

The inquisitive Fusher made a practice of rubbing elbows
with celebrities. He wanted to be known as a regular member of the unregistered club of the intelligentsia. The habit
gave zest to his life, and was good for his business. To sit
alone in the coffee-house was boring, but to drink tea and
nod familiarly to an artist or writer or actor sitting at another table, and then to go over to him and speak of the
weather or of a play or of a book, made the tea that you
absorbed taste ever so much better. He was the advertizing
agent of a monthly publication. He sold opera tickets at a
discount. He knew where the best pawnshops were located,
and could be of service in many other ways.

He met Manewitz for the first time in the office of his
magazine, and nodded to him. Then he met him in a restaurant and, introducing himself as an admirer of Russian
literature, invited Manewitz to have tea with him. Manewitz stared at him, and was about to give a growl of contempt; but he felt like having a glass of tea, so he sat down
with him and listened to his foolish chatter for a while. That
incident gave Fusher the right to call Manewitz his friend,
and soon he was a frequent visitor at Manewitz's home. In
the course of conversation he mentioned the Yiddish theatre.

"Why haven't you ever written a play, Gospodin Mane-witz?" he asked. "I can't understand why you should go to the foreign market to sell the things you write, when right here, under your nose, you have a world you could conquer."

"I never thought of it," said Manewitz.

"Take me, for instance," said Fusher. "I have written God knows how many plays. I know dramatic technique like a typesetter his type. But the theatre is so ignorant that I can't even get a hearing. When I show Burlak one of my plays, he tells me it lacks the Lecker touch. Isn't that disgusting?"

"Do you mean that scribbler who writes endless novels for the *Tageblatt*?" asked Manewitz.

"That's the man," said Fusher.

"They ought to stuff his *romanen* down his throat and choke him," said Manewitz.

Manewitz had never written a play. He was not interested in the theatre. He did not absorb life through his eyes. He heard things, he used his mind, his sense of smell, his sense of touch, but not his eyes. He read plays as he read novels. He thought of the theatre as a bastard art. The play had no existence of its own; it was made by the director, the actors, the scene-painters, the musicians, and finally by the audience. Without these auxiliary arts, the play was a dead thing. It had to be made to live after it was written. The playwright was merely the initiator of the play. But Manewitz was not too old to learn, and if, as Fusher said, there was a living to be made at writing plays, he intended to find out about the matter.

He discovered a short story among his manuscripts. It told of the experiences of a Russian immigrant on the East Side. It contained episodes in a sweatshop, dealt with adjustments to customs, language, and social relations. He wrote the play as fast as his pen could cover paper, drinking gallons of tea, smoking endless cigarettes. He gave no thought to scenery, divisions into acts, to actors or managers. It was a fresh, highly colored play; the dialogue was simple and natural; there was no singing or dancing. It was just a play.

When the last word had been written, Manewitz sent for Fusher, went to the bureau, produced the manuscript and said:

"Listen! I wrote this play to show you that writing a play is a simple exercise in composition. If a man has a story to tell, it can be told in the form of a play, too. Here it is."

"I knew you could do it," said Fusher, beaming. He read a few scenes, fingered the book and then asked, disturbed:

"Who is the leading character?"

"Why should there be a leading character? One is as good as another. In fact, I like best that little fellow in the shop; he hasn't much to say, but he's very interesting and funny."

"But I ask you, if a play has no leading character, who is to play it? If the woman leads, then you have Madame Lessin. If the man is the hero, big and strong, then it's Burlak. If it's a character part, there's Ritter.

"You're talking in riddles," said Manewitz, "What have I got to do with this Lessin and Burlak and Ritter? All these parts are in my play. What difference does it make?"

"What are you saying, Gospodin? In every play only one star is possible. No more. There are three companies and three managers who are the stars. You must make your choice. Unless that is done, I don't see what can be done about it."

Manewitz glared at Fusher, took the manuscript from him, and replaced it carefully in the bureau.

"You are no better than the rest of them," he said. "You

tell me of things that have nothing to do with plays. I think
of a play and you think of a theatre. I think of a play and
you think of stars. I have never had my manuscripts edited,
and I don't propose having that done to any play I write.
Please get out of my house. I'm ashamed I ever spoke to a
man like you."

Fusher left the house, humiliated, and Manewitz turned
to other matters. He decided that he had wasted his time.
The play was returned to the morgue, in which reposed
many other articles and stories, many other unprofitable
ideas. Some months later, when Manewitz had forgotten the
incident, he met Fusher and was about to pass him by. But
Fusher was not proud, Fusher was not abashed. He had all
the brazenness of an advertizing agent. He turned around
and walked with Manewitz.

"How is the play getting on?" he asked.

Manewitz said nothing but walked faster. "Don't dog my
steps," he said.

"You have a wrong idea of me, Gospodin Manewitz,"
Fusher said breathlessly, walking fast to keep up with Manewitz. "I am just as interested in literature as you are. Haven't
I written plays that they have refused to look at? Have I
ever debased my art—have you ever seen a play of mine in
the Yiddish theatre? I am giving you the advice of a good
friend. I give you the benefit of my experience. Take it or
leave it, but don't insult me."

"Well, let that go. What do you want now?" asked Manewitz. He did not harbor a grudge for long. The agitation
of Fusher interested him. He understood the little people of
the earth, the dwarfed and frustrated, those who were pushed
about, the defeated who made the best of their defeat by
adjusting themselves to the world in which they lived.

"Let me have your manuscript, Gospodin Manewitz, and

I assure you I'll try to sell it for you," said Fusher. "I'll
do my best to introduce literature in the Yiddish theatre.
They'll take it as it is or I won't give it to them."

"Well, have it your way. I depend upon you," said Manewitz. He let Fusher have the manuscript.

Fusher decided he would see Burlak first. He went about
the task with forethought. He invited Burlak to dine at the
Café Boulevard. He used the time Burlak gave to his food
to deliver a discourse on realism. Out of politeness—Fusher
was host—Burlak grunted his comments and went on dis-
posing of his food, saying very little. Finally, when black
coffee arrived and he was smoking his cigar, Burlak said:

"You've said enough, Fusher, stop! The play's not for me,
you know what I mean. I need something that I can build
up—on what the dramatist writes. Now, there's Ritter. He
might make something of it with spotlights and melodrama.
He knows the tricks. But you know me. I'm playing Lecker's
trash, and that keeps me busy. And more than that, I've
heard of this Manewitz. He's a regular barbarian. He thinks
he can get by with a big voice and heavy fist. He has the
manners of a gangster, and I don't want to have anything
to do with him."

Fusher called for the bill and looked at it sadly. So much
money wasted. It was worth something giving Burlak a lec-
ture on realism, but not that much. He could have given
the same discourse in a coffee-house to more intelligent
listeners. That was that. He would have to see Ritter next.
With the aid of Goulash, Ritter's factotum, he arranged to
have the imposing tragedian come to Lorber's, and there
Fusher sat, awaiting his arrival, the manuscript flat on the
table.

Before Ritter sat down, he disposed of his fur coat, adjusted his glasses, put his gold-headed cane in a safe corner,

called the waiter and ordered a glass of milk. He gave whispered instructions to Goulash, who left at once. And then he said:

"Why have you dragged me here, Mr. Fusher?"

"You are the only man with vision. You are not afraid to tackle the new things. I have a new play by a new writer. The man who introduces him to the Jewish people will make theatre history. He is a distinguished literary man."

"What do you mean by literary?" asked Ritter, who hated the word. To him it meant slavish adherence to a text. Such plays always hampered his style. "Haven't we enough of literature? I hear the word so often it makes me sick. There is Uriel Acosta and Don Carlos, and look what a failure Tolstoy's 'Power of Darkness' was."

"But this is literature in a realistic setting, with Jewish taste," said Fusher. "There are no long speeches. It's the language of the common people. The dialogue is superb. Hauptmann could not do better. The leading part is like it was made for you. Even Burlak admits it."

"To whom did that scoundrel say that?" said Ritter, complacently.

"When I told him the plot a week ago," said Fusher, "that teamster couldn't read Manewitz's writing, but he admitted it was not for him."

Ritter fingered the manuscript without interest.

"I don't know this fellow. Who is Manewitz?" he asked.

While Fusher dilated on the genius of Manewitz, Ritter seemed to be glancing through the pages of the manuscript.

"I don't think this play is what I want," he said finally, calling for his fur coat. "This fellow may be a good writer, but he don't know the theatre. He's a *yold*, like all of them. And look at the cast of characters! I'd have to have an army to play it."

"Now you're joking," said Fusher.

"I'll tell you, Mr. Fusher," said Ritter, now fully attired, with fur coat, hat, cane, and eyeglasses. "I have no use for it, but to show you my respect for literature, and to encourage this amateur, knowing full well that to put it on the stage I'll have to get somebody to fix it—say Solatev—I'll take it off your hands and give you, say, sixty-five dollars. Take it or leave it."

"Let me thank you," Fusher hurried to say, shaking Ritter's hand. "But make it seventy-five dollars and the play is yours."

"Call at my cashier's office tomorrow and he will give you what I promised," said Ritter, stuffing the manuscript in his overcoat pocket.

Elated, Fusher rushed over to Manewitz's the next day, laid a wad of bills on the writing desk, counted seventy-five dollars with great deliberation, and pushed the bills toward Manewitz, who was writing. Manewitz looked at the display of wealth and calmly asked:

"What for?"

"For the play, Gospodin Manewitz. What did I tell you? Ritter has an eye for genius. He has taken the play and will play it in due course," said Fusher, excited, dancing about the room.

Manewitz put the money in his pocket, rewarded Fusher with a broad smile, and patted him on the back.

"I thought you were a bluffer, but the money speaks for itself," he said, and returned to his desk. There was an article he had to finish for the next foreign mail.

Ritter went about the work of producing the new play in the usual way. He first saw to it that music was provided here and there, as was the custom. He ordered a popular song for the comedian. He favored the leading actress with a solo number in the first act. He had a few chorus numbers thrown in as an emergency measure. He sent for a scene-painter. He went about thinking how he would make up in the new part. Ritter had no need for the author when he began rehearsal of the new play. The play belonged to him, and he could do with it as he pleased. The players were not required to be letter perfect in their parts. It was enough if they were familiar with the business in hand. What was important was the accessories—the exits and entrances, the dispositions of the pieces of scenery, and the special scenes in which he himself would have the center of the stage. What did the authors know about their plays? What did they know of the theatre? The less one saw of them the better for the play.

Fusher was only invited to stay away from the rehearsals. He was eager to see what had been made of his friend's composition. He would have regarded it as an honor to be allowed to look in, but had to content himself with snatched words with the actors as they emerged from the rehearsals.

He was told by Simonov, one of the older actors:

"The like of this play I have never heard or seen. It's going to ruin the theatre. Such Yiddish you never heard out of the mouth of a Jew. Where he got his characters, God alone could tell, and worse than that, it's full of *rishus*. When the Jews see it, they will tear the theatre apart."

First performances in those days went unnoticed. Critics did not come until they were invited. Their invitations were timed to coincide with special advertisements in the newspapers. News of the new plays seeped into the editorial offices, and reviews were considered a form of reading notice. Why should the theatre be given any more free publicity than a department store? Special inducements had to be offered to a member of a newspaper staff to waste his time seeing a play and then writing about it.

The author of the new play knew nothing of the production

until Fusher came to invite him to the first performance.
At first he refused. He would see it some other time. The
play did not interest him. But Fusher persuaded him that it
was customary for the author to be present in case the audience called for him—either to applaud or to hiss.

When Manewitz came to the theatre it was crowded to
the rafters. Ritter had filled the gallery with friends of proved
ability as hand-clappers and cheerers. The orchestra was less
liberally patronized. The curtain was slow in rising. The
gallery became impatient. Finally, the orchestra appeared and
the play began.

Manewitz sat stolidly through the first acts of the performances. He seemed deep in thought. He did not move
when the audience shouted its approval. But in the middle
of the last act he rose, motioned to Fusher, and asked him
the way to the stage. Fusher supposed that Manewitz knew
of the custom of calling for the author, and that he was
prepared to acknowledge the applause and even to make
a speech. As they walked to the stage, Fusher said excitedly:
"Remember, make the speech short."

Together they waited in the wings for the curtain to fall.
As Ritter left the stage, he was attired as an old man. Manewitz came forward, and without any introduction, grabbed
him by the collar and shook him until every bone in his
body rattled. He shouted in Russian, which few of the audience understood.

"What in hell does this mean?" Ritter spluttered. His
beard was in disorder and his wig was shaken off, and he
could hardly catch his breath.

"You fraud—you botcher!" exclaimed Manewitz, as he
continued to shake the actor. "I'll break every bone in your
body. Satisfaction—I demand satisfaction!"

The attack on Ritter drew a crowd of actors around him,

but they could not break Manewitz's hold. He dragged Ritter with him about the stage. The applause out front continued, for the audience expected Ritter to appear and say a few words. They wanted to greet him and the company, and cheer them. This Ritter was conscious of as he struggled with Manewitz. Finally he extricated himself and shouted at his assailant:

"What satisfaction—for what?"

"I want you to go out and tell the audience that the words of those songs—the idea of having songs altogether—are not the author's, but were written by a bastard who hasn't an idea or a tune in his head. I want them to know that the jokes of that scarecrow of a comedian were not mine. It's humiliating to have such trash presented as if I had written it. If you don't go out and do this, I promise you I'll do it myself."

The crowd burst out laughing. Ritter himself felt as if a load had been removed from his shoulders. He thought that a maniac had broken into the theatre and was intent on destroying him.

"This is the funniest thing I have ever heard of," he said. "The *yold*. He must be the author!"

Then, gathering strength, he stood up and took Manewitz's hand.

"Why didn't you tell me what you wanted? Glad to meet you, Mr. Manewitz. I'll not only tell them what you want, but I'll have a few complimentary words to say about you too."

The impatient audience was soon duly informed in German-Yiddish hyperbole (mock humility and discreet brag) that credit for the magnificent play that they had seen must be given where credit is due. The gems of song that they had heard were written by the world-renowned folk-singer,

Schmulevitz, who could always be relied upon to evoke the authentic sentiments of every true Jewish heart. To the ingenious, talented, well-beloved comedian, Lazar Badchen, must go credit for their enjoyment of the humorous sallies, the laughable jests, the grotesque antics and the dances they had heard and seen. For all the rest, they must express their gratitude to a promising author whom he (Ritter) had had the good fortune to discover and to introduce to the Yiddish theatre. This was his first good play, and he could assure them that the next one—if he ever came to write it, and if God would only inspire him to write it—would be an even better play.

That was how Manewitz arrived. He was the first writer for the Yiddish theatre who had the will and the physical strength to break the bones of any actor or manager who interfered with the text of his plays. If God had not given him this strength and courage, the new drama would never have found a place in the Yiddish theatre.

Not that his victory was won on that first night. To ensure the performance of his plays as written, he would drop in at rehearsals and performances without notice. He would sit unseen in a box, like a watchful shadow, and when the actors wandered from their text, he would suddenly rise out of the darkness and tell them what he thought of them in good, racy Russian. His Russian sounded more ferocious to those who did not understand it than to those who did. He barked, he growled, he threatened. The actors never knew when he would appear to check up on them. It is recorded that he once reproved Dikman at a rehearsal for introducing his own material. Dikman shouted back at him:

"What right has the author to tell me what words I shall speak in any part I condescend to play? The part is mine, and I know what should be said."

Manewitz smacked his face, and left the theatre. He used the incident in a feuilleton to tell his readers of the low mentality of the Yiddish acting fraternity. Once he sat in an orchestra, taking a vacant seat, and when Lazar Badchen least expected it, stood up to tell him:

"Don't be a buffoon! If you keep this up any longer, I'll thrash you within an inch of your life!"

Badchen was so frightened that he ran into the wings and hid himself in his dressing-room.

Soon they learned that it was wiser to play straight than to stray from the text. It was agreed that when you played Manewitz, you had to listen to the prompter. That was one of the sacrifices you had to make for the literary drama. You enjoyed your freedom in one of the *shund* plays. But Manewitz made you suffer the discipline of higher art. There was money to be made in Lecker's melodramas, but you made your reputation in Manewitz's. Madame Lessin devoted herself exclusively to Manewitz's plays. That, they said, was why she had a great reputation but was always broke.

But Manewitz's way to fame was dogged by Fusher, who followed him in loyal self-interest, not only as disciple, but as discoverer. It was he who had made a new epoch in the Yiddish theatre possible. It was his advance publicity, his persuasion of Ritter, his tact, his modesty, his devotion, that had produced Manewitz. He did not intend to let the world forget it, so he wrote it down in a book. Nor did he let Manewitz forget it, ever.

VI

Madame Weisl's Husband

LEON WEISL WAS A PUNY MAN WITH SMALL EYES, A PROMINENT
nose, and puffed out cheeks. His voice was shrill, and he
could sing falsetto without giving himself a pain. He could
be called an actor. He loved fine clothes, and would spend
his last rouble for fancy vests, neckties, and handkershiefs.
Never being in the money, he would occasionally appear
with a new high hat, but with his trousers frayed at the
edges; or with a Prince Albert coat and a shabby hat or
torn shoes.

During his younger days as an actor he met in Vilna a
young salesgirl whom, in a moment of romantic ardor, he
made his wife. For all stage purposes the girl had no name,
so that from the moment of her introduction to theatrical
life she was merely Weisl's wife. She was bright and clever,
and knew something of life. She married Weisl because he
gave her an outlet to a freer existence. Her youth had been
made unhappy by a brutal father. As the wife of an actor
she was soon assigned a thinking part in one play, a small

speaking part in another; then she did odd jobs for the stock company for general purposes. Weisl's clothes, his cigarettes, his voice, were of the stage; why not his wife?

By a trick of fortune Madame Weisl was given a part in one of the Manewitz dramas of which the Russian strolling players had not as yet given unauthorized performances. Manewitz at that time was merely a name. His plays were talked about, but seldom played. It was only after a few of the actors of Second Avenue had returned to Russia with stolen prompt-books that Manewitz become a reality. The play Weisl's company appropriated had a tragic part for a woman, and as it was that of an old woman the leading lady refused to play it—she was at least forty-five—so the part was given to Madame Weisl, who was at least twenty-five.

A critic of Russian literature who dabbled in the drama (behind the scenes), was present in the small theatre where the play was being given, and reviewed the playing and the play. Madame Weisl had made a deep impression upon him. Gossip said that the impression was based more on intimacy than convention allowed. Subrassov was a massive man with imposing whiskers who wrote in Russian, and for a Yiddish player to be praised in a Russian journal was an indication that the Chosen People had once more been discovered. Madame Weisl's reputation was made. Subrassov subsequently had a falling-out with the star he had made and tried to tear down what he had built up, but the idea had become fixed that Madame Weisl was the greatest Russian-Yiddish actress, and there it stayed. Madame Weisl stood in the theatrical firmament, as it were, on her own legs (which the Jewish public, unfortunately, had never seen), and the status of Weisl was threatened. In the twinkling of an eye, he became Madame Weisl's husband.

The fame of Madame Weisl extended to New York, where

at that time everything with a Russian label was acclaimed. Evidence of intellectual superiority was indicated by local depreciation and super-appreciation of foreign goods. Soon the radical press on the Yiddish Rialto rang with the praises of the new star. Madame Lessin was relegated to the background for the time being, and other actresses, soubrettes, heavy women, and what not, who had received their acclaim only in New York, were treated with a lofty disdain.

Burlak was on the lookout one season for some means of sticking a knife through the fifth rib of Ritter, whose competition was depleting his treasury. Something must be done to reduce that star to his proper commercial importance. Burlak sent an emissary to Vilna to treat with Madame Weisl, to lay before her an alluring picture of the rewards that awaited her in the American Ghetto. His emissary encountered Weisl himself, and at once felt that he was in the presence of a difficulty. The husband of a star actress is excess baggage. Whatever he may be, he is not an advantage. (Witness the husband of the noted beauty, Madame Fishkind; it was her husband who prevented a unanimous paean of praise; he was always in the way; his name stood out and protruded at times when it had been necessary to let Madame Fishkind shine alone. There must be some trace of the hetaera in an actress to make her the object of general masculine attraction, without which stars are not made. The presence of Fishkind destroyed the illusion of the general accessibility of Madame—although that accessibility was more fiction than fact.) At any rate, Burlak's emissary cabled to his chief that a husband of the Weisl was in the way. The emissary received a reply which, translated into Broadway patois, meant smother the husband.

The emissary was a stocky young man named Todres, who had become a lawyer to please his father, a retired

Yiddish actor (retired to the wilds of New Jersey, where he had a chicken farm), but who had always been attracted to the stage. It was a biological urge. After a practice of five or six years he found himself with Yiddish actors and actresses as his only clients, which meant that he knew penury intimately. But he was practiced in the ways of stars and of women (and of the husbands of actresses with whom he played cards.)

His terms for Madame Weisl were, translated into rouble values, astounding. Weisl was gratified and Madame Weisl was almost prostrated. They had been playing for years and had barely met expenses. Poverty was always lurking around the corner, even when they rolled in temporary luxury.

"What guarantee have we," said Weisl, when he had recovered his composure, "that Burlak will pay the salary?"

"I have orders to deposit at your banker's the sum of one thousand dollars as a guarantee of good faith," replied Todres.

"How much more will you give for my services?" asked Weisl. "I also am a star actor."

"That," Todres hastened to say, "is a matter which we shall have to discuss further."

"What do you mean?" asked Madame Weisl, glancing anxiously at her spouse.

"We must first agree as to Madame's salary, sign the contract, then we shall proceed further," said Todres.

When Weisl approached Todres to adjust the second contract he found that gentleman contemplating a Yiddish newspaper and puffing away at a cigarette.

"Well, my good friend Todres," he began, "I am prepared to talk business with you."

"I have just received a cablegram from Burlak," said Todres.

"I am glad to hear it," said Weisl. "What is the news?"

"It is necessary, for reasons I cannot go into," said Todres, "that Madame Weisl come to New York without her husband."

Weisl arose, his face flushed.

"Madame Weisl goes nowhere without me," he stammered. "And I resent this sort of American business. Without me Madame Weisl is nothing. I am her husband, her comrade, her partner, you understand?"

Todres hastened to appease the enraged artist.

"I do not mean that you are not to accompany her," he said, "but you must not appear on the stage while Madame Weisl is with us. She must come to New York not only as an actress, but as a beautiful woman. You are not acquainted with the ways of America. A woman on the stage may be married, but it must not be forced upon the attention of the public. The public likes to know that the idols of the stage are free. A husband in the same company, on the same stage, in the same city, would spoil everything."

Weisl fumed and threatened and pleaded. Madame Weisl saw the princely fortune offered to her melt away in the heat of Weisl's anger. But Weisl himself had no desire to lose what represented as much money as he and his wife could earn in ten years.

It was finally decided that Weisl should come to New York with his wife and for at least two months remain incognito. He was to be his wife's manager, but not an actor. Should the opportunity arise, he might be permitted to appear in special performances.

No mention was made in New York of the husband of the beautiful, eccentric Madame Weisl, the successor of Madame Duse and the compeer of Madame Bernhardt. Placards proclaimed her beauty and her success. Her picture, modified by artists of the East Side, decorated the walls of dilapidated buildings. Criticisms from Russian newspapers were reprinted, but nowhere was there any mention of Leon Weisl. The Yiddish Rialto did not know of his existence.

For weeks Madame Weisl was engaged with dressmakers. She dreamed of conquering the New World, and of making a name for herself that would invade Russia with the accumulated momentum of a European journey; and she did not give much thought to Weisl. She was his wife, but between them there had been the utmost freedom. She was loyal to the partnership, loyal to his interests, and there would never be any scandal.

Imagine New York—the Yiddish Rialto—in a mood of expectation, preparing to greet a new reigning actress. There were the preliminary puffs in the press, the many-colored advance posters, the busy conversation in the coffee-houses, the excited comments of the intelligentsia. (That strange word intelligentsia! It covered a world of pompous ignorance. It signified the intellectual snob, the literary parvenu, the pretense and humbug of intellectual vagabondage.) For years there had been nothing new on the Yiddish stage. Always the same old faces, always the same old mannerisms; the habitués could identify the actors with eyes closed. Women who had come into their own as sylph-like creatures had acquired a heaviness which only outsiders saw. Men who had made themselves famous as lovers were now bulky and middle-aged. The chorus girls whose youth had appealed to the generation of twenty-five years ago (or had they ever been youthful?) now came to the theatre accompanied by their grandchildren. There was nothing of the unexpected there. All dull, prosaic, common, routine.

Now, hail to Madame Weisl, stage beauty, great actress, eccentric, full of wit and repartee, a fresh face, young, ingenious, European—that was the story of the press agent. She would outshine the great actresses of the American stage. A new thing in Yiddish circles, thank God, something to be admired and feted, to give one a feeling of youth, to overthrow the mustiness that had accumulated in the Yiddish stage. Tear away the traditions—give the old routine the boot—tell Ritter and his routinized bluff and Burlak with his roarings that their glory has passed, and the torch has been taken by younger hands. Hail to Madame Weisl!

Madame Weisl was beseiged at the dock by a group of newspaper men, who saw before them a demure, well-kept, hearty young woman, with deep black eyes, a strong contralto voice, animated, well-dressed, speaking Yiddish with a delightful accent. What she said was jotted down. Her picture was snapped. Her gestures were described. She was asked questions about the status of European drama, her friendship with the great Russian actress, Madame Komisarzhevsky and her escapades; but no one took any notice of Leon Weisl, who stood by holding several bundles, one of them containing the press notices his wife had received in St. Petersburg. (And also a larger bundle of clippings of his own.)

He was introduced as her manager. It was assumed that he was her brother. Todres was at the dock and prevented him from joining in the conversation, interrupting him when he approached the danger line, and effectively diverting him from all efforts at getting his name in the newspapers. The interviews were edited; Weisl's name, even as a brother, was kept out, and Madame Weisl entered New York as a lady unencumbered.

At the hotel a suite of rooms was engaged, a maid was

secured, and Weisl was assigned to one of the rooms. He thought this an American custom, and was too timid to ask any questions on such a delicate matter.

Madame Weisl appeared on the stage two weeks later, and made a deep impression upon a large audience. So carefully had the Weisl sentiment been worked up that there was not a dissenting voice in the chorus of approval. Madame Weisl was everything it had been said she was, and more. As a foreigner she had the additional charm of an exotic plant, while her Yiddish, so clean-cut, lacking the mannerisms of New York's Ghetto, charmed the audience, brought something into their lives that reminded them of home.

Some weeks later there were rumors that Madame Weisl had a husband, a small, insignificant man, who claimed to be an actor, and who insisted that he had trained Madame Weisl, that he had given her the experience which had made possible her success. He was reported to have said, furthermore, that if he were given a chance he would show Burlak and Ritter and the entire Actors' Union that the Yiddish actors from home, like all else in Jewish life that came from Lithuania, had a tang and a quality beyond compare.

The rumors had emanated from Weisl himself, who was envious of his wife's success. Every round of applause she received cut him to the quick. He saw her surrounded by admirers, her name spread over billboards in large show cards. Her art was admired, her beauty was praised. It was predicted that America would never let her go. An attempt was being made to give special performances of European plays in a Broadway theatre, and he, Weisl, who had made her what she was, was cast ignominiously into the shade. He had to prevaricate about his identity. He had to remain in obscurity in order that she might shine alone. He did not begrudge Madame Weisl any of the praise accorded her, but he wanted to show these American yokels that he, too, could act. But there was the contract in which he had agreed to remain unemployed. The season was well advanced now, and he could not secure a regular engagement. So he contented himself for the time being with telling a few people who he was. These few people circulated the information, and the Rialto soon knew that Madame Weisl, the great beauty and artiste, was married to an actor named Weisl, a shrimp of a man who wore spats and displayed peculiarly loud neckties.

Todres had a conference with Weisl.

"How is this, Weisl!" he exclaimed in anger. "Do you want to spoil your wife's engagement? You see how well she has taken here. There are thousands of dollars in this for both of you. When the New York engagement is finished we shall take her on the road. There are millions on the road, for her with the notoriety we have given her. Do you want to spoil all this?"

"What good does it do me if my wife makes a name for herself?" said Weisl moodily. "It's my name, and I won't let anybody—not even my wife—rob me of it. I am an artist, too. My life depends upon acting. You can't keep me locked up here, and sentenced to sit day in and day out listening to the applause given to my wife, who, let me tell you, I myself trained."

"You may be an actor," said Todres, "but you can't deliver the goods."

"What do you mean?" exclaimed Weisl.

"I mean that no matter how good an actor you may be, no one will take you at your word. There must be publicity first, then ability. First press-agenting, then acting. Do you think Madame Weisl would have made such a furore if it hadn't been for what we had done in the press before she came? Let me tell you, my friend," said Todres, biting savagely at a Pittsburgh stogie, "you don't exist here. You are a dead one. So keep quiet, if you know on which side your bread is buttered."

Weisl said nothing. His small eyes were fired with determination, however, and Todres left him with a feeling that the man was dangerous. He so reported to Burlak.

"Let him try any of his monkeyshines on me," said Burlak, "and I'll cut Madame Weisl off in the middle of the season. I don't care what happens."

Burlak himself was disturbed by Madame Weisl's success. It was true that he was her manager and that whatever profit there was would go to him, but Burlak was also an actor, and he could not bear the tremendous success of his co-star. While he would not do anything to jeopardize that success, he would not have taken amiss an opportunity again to hold the center of the stage alone.

Madame Weisl was in a state of continous excitement. Her success intoxicated her. She could speak of nothing else. She nagged Weisl at breakfast with her reports of what this man or that man had said to her. Weisl was compelled to listen to her talk and not show his displeasure. He smiled and swallowed his bile.

Some of Madame Weisl's admirers became persistent. They took her for drives, they showered her with presents. It was said that the cashier of the theatre was specially attentive, and Burlak set an extra guard on the cashbox. A prominent East Side attorney was smitten with such a passion that he hovered about Madame Weisl's hotel all day long, and it appeared to Weisl that she was not averse to his attentions. As a result there were soon many quarrels between them, and within a few weeks they had ceased to be on speaking terms.

On one of the side streets there was a small theatre which was now a music hall. At one time a troupe of Russian players, headed by that eccentric genius Paul Orleneff, had given performances in it for several months. Weisl learned that the music hall was about to be abandoned, and he put himself in touch with the lessees.

Todres rushed into Burlak's office in a fury of excitement.

"Have you seen what that scoundrel of a Weisl has done?" he exclaimed.

"Skipped to Russia, I bet," said Burlak.

"Read this," said Todres, handing him a poster.

The poster read that Leon Weisl, husband of Madame Weisl, who had made such a tremendous success at Burlak's theatre, would appear with a company of extraordinary players for a season of four weeks in repertoire.

"The rascal!" said Burlak, crumpling the poster. "He comes here every Saturday night, gets his wife's money, and then has the audacity to start competing with us. We must have it out with him."

"I'll get out an injunction," said Todres. "What do you say?"

Burlak shook his head.

"Don't get out any injunctions," he said. "I'll see Madame Weisl, and tell her that if her husband appears anywhere I'll take twenty per cent from her salary, and then let her sue me."

When Todres told this to Madame Weisl she turned pale. Deduct twenty per cent from her salary? Weisl was consuming the greater part of her income. He left her just enough to get along on. If it had not been for the presents

she was receiving she would have been penniless. She sent
for Weisl, and he came to her room.

"What's this I hear about your appearance on the stage
here?" she said.

"What you have heard is correct," said Weisl coolly.

"Have you forgotten the agreement I have with Burlak?"
she said.

"I have not forgotten it," said Weisl, keeping his temper
down.

"Why do you do this then? Do you want to jeopardize
my position here, and do you want me to lose everything
I have gained by being thrown out in the middle of the
season?" she said with feeling.

"That's just it," he said, rising. "You think only of yourself. I was an artist before you ever went on the stage. I
married you and made you what you are. Now you want me
to be eclipsed by you. You want me to sit in a hole like a
dog tied to his kennel, while you reap all the honors. I
will not do it. I cannot endure this any longer. For six
weeks now I have kept quiet. I have seen you dragged
around town by your admirers. No one knows me. No one
cares for me. For my own honor I must refuse to become a
hanger-on to your fortunes. It is not the money that counts.
Nor is it the success that you have made, nor the money
that counts with you."

Madame Weisl, drawing the skirt of her fashionable gown
about her and touching her hips in the old fashion, also rose.

"By that last sentence you mean——" she said, with a
rising reflection.

"I mean that you are receiving the attentions of that
fellow Borsuk too eagerly. I don't like it," said Weisl.

"Well, if you don't like it, you are at liberty to do as you please about it," was the reply of the lady whom Weisl had made a star actress.

In fact, she was rather tired of Weisl. The American style of living attracted her. She felt that her husband was useless in this bustling metropolis, and inasmuch as the ties that united them had always been of the freest, she felt that frankness on her part was desirable, especially as Borsuk, the energetic East Side lawyer, was becoming desperate in his attentions, and he was not such a bad fellow, after all.

A break with Weisl just now would not be to her disadvantage anywhere but in her business relations with Burlak. As a successful actress in America, with a man like Borsuk in her train, she could easily make her way unaided by a man whose only function was that of a collector. She could collect her salary herself, even if Burlak deducted the twenty per cent.

"That has been your aim all along," exclaimed Weisl. "Now that you have a position here, you think you can get along without me. Let me tell you, then, that I, too, can get along without you. I shall be the bearer of the name Weisl, and I shall make as good an impression here as an actor as you have, without stooping to such tricks as getting men to pay me attentions for the sake of what they give me. You are no better than when I married you. Then you were a salesgirl, with a pretty face and admirers; now you are on the stage, where everyone can see your beauty and if necessary pay a little more. Your value now is due to me, but the kind of value is the same as before."

With that Weisl left her, left the hotel, and with the few hundred dollars he had in hand, prepared for his first appearance.

The news that Leon Weisl was to appear for the first time attracted a large first-night audience. Madame Weisl's reputation helped Weisl. He was Madame Weisl's husband, and it was said by enemies of Burlak in the employ of Ritter that it was Weisl who had made the name of Weisl famous, not Madame Weisl.

The play was an old-fashioned Russian one, which Weisl himself had adapted. It was stilted and draggy, with no climaxes, and with a part in which Weisl appeared as an old man. He considered himself the best player of old men on the Yiddish stage. But as his luck would have it, a young man in the company, previously unknown and without employment, made a deep impression in the part of the young lover. Try as he would, Weisl could not overcome this disadvantage. Krantz was the hero of the evening, and Weisl was left in the shade. His voice was monotonous, his manners were awkward, and he knew little or nothing of the methods in vogue on the Yiddish stage in America.

The press pointed out his faults and deplored the fact that a man of such mediocre talents should announce himself as a star when a second-rate actor like Krantz could outshine him. Even the partisans of Ritter could not find a word of praise for Weisl. In the second performance of the same play he took away the part of the young lover from Krantz and essayed it himself, but the public now saw Krantz in the part of the old man, and the comparison was not to Weisl's advantage.

The little theatre on the side street closed within two weeks, and Weisl's dream of conquering the New World was exploded. His conduct toward Madame Weisl was such that she now refused to see him, and he had to shift for himself. Wherever he went people pointed at him, saying, "There goes Madame Weisl's husband." He was not himself any more than he had been before. To add to his wretchedness, Madame Weisl issued a statement that she intended to remain in the United States. A resourceful reporter added that she would soon obtain a divorce from Weisl. Meanwhile, Borsuk's attentions continued.

Weisl was embittered. While his money lasted he was bold and vituperative. He declared that he would contest the divorce suit. He hinted darkly that he would bring a countersuit. He even threatened to levy an attachment on Burlak's cash box and claim Madame Weisl's salary. But as his funds ran out, he felt that he must do something to reconcile himself with the situation, so he made overtures to Madame Weisl, to which she refused to listen. He remained in New York until he had only a few dollars left, and then appealed to his wife for passage money to Russia, which she gave him on one condition—that he would never trouble her again. He left, and never troubled her again.

Several months after Weisl left, Madame Weisl secured her divorce and was promptly married to the prominent attorney who had been her protector and guide. With a reputation assured, and with a husband capable of supporting her in case of need, Madame Weisl had no trouble in making her way. The only difference was that Borsuk played no part in his own name. He had become a part of his wife's entourage. He stood in her shadow. The name Borsuk was effaced. So far as the public was concerned, he did not exist. He was merely the husband of Madame Weisl.

VII

Breaking the Triangle

"WHAT HAS BECOME OF THAT LITTLE SOUBRETTE KAMENETZ?"
I asked Simonov during a conversation at his home.

Simonov has long passed his youth; he has settled down
as a resident actor, and lives in a flat in Harlem. He never
talks of becoming a "star" or a manager. He is just an actor.
He plays the season, carries a few dollars each week to the
bank against the day of days when he will have to say
good-bye to the stage, and lives the life of a staid burgher.
He has no prejudices. He praises the successful, laments with
the failures, and has a reputation for discretion, which makes
him the confidant of many of his comrades. You may be
sure that his appetite is good and that he sleeps well. When
he tells a story he is not subject to the malicious backbiting
common to actors, who, while they praise, tear at the heart
of the thing by cunning innuendo.

That was why I asked him of La Belle Kamenetz. I had
already heard the testimony of gossip. I pretended to com-

105

plete ignorance about the affair which had caused such a stir at the time on the Yiddish Rialto.

Simonov invited me into his parlor, which was decorated with pictures of himself in many poses. He closed the folding doors behind him, thus shutting out his wife, a good, home-loving person who, though familiar with the ways of actors, "need not hear this story over again," said Simonov, apologetically.

"No, Kamenetz is not on Broadway," he said, "although she might have been there had she wanted to. She is now retired, and the cause of her retirement may interest you. I knew her and her husband. I suppose you have heard how Kamenetz made his final exit. It was his first appearance in a star part, but he got little enjoyment out of it, the poor wretch.

"Kamenetz played in the Yiddish theatres for years before they found him out. He was a medium-sized man with a heavy, inexpressive face and a voice that was rough and harsh in the places where it wasn't cracked. He never learned how to make up, he could not sing or dance, yet he was reckoned as an actor in the old country for years. He was found out when he came to New York. You see how far the Yiddish stage has progressed. Over there, Kamenetz was a *macher*; here, he was properly cut out of the cast of characters, eliminated from all stock companies, and was reduced within a few years to the position of a hanger-on, a man who took odd jobs in the acting line, from cutting capers in a music hall to bumming his way through the provinces with a strolling company.

"It was his good fortune to marry well. He picked up Bessie Fonarof, a young girl of the chorus. It wasn't considered a brilliant match at the time, for who expected anything from the row of dames who make up the chorus of a Yiddish theatre? But Bessie was the exception. When Kamenetz was looking around for a stray job, Bessie emerged from the chorus and made a hit as a soubrette, and it was up to Kamenetz to look sharp in order to keep up his end of the partnership.

"Bessie was about fifteen years his junior, and his opposite in every respect. She was vivacious, generous, whole-souled, while he was taciturn, secretive, and of a mean disposition. If ever there was love between them, it got lost in the scuffle of theatrical life. He was a curious specimen. He loved her, but it was the love of a middle-aged man for his chattel, and once having hitched her up in his stall, he didn't trouble much about thieves. He had something of the old-fashioned bourgeois in him, although his life had been spent as a vagabond. It is a reversion to type, as the books say, for a Jew to become bourgeois. That is his natural state.

"Bessie probably married him because there was nobody else in sight, and she was young. She was ignorant of life, and he was an actor, while she was in the chorus. But she saw how much out of place he was in the theatre, and after she had become a mother, and had seen a little of life, there was no reason why she should remain with him except out of regard for her children, and because of that strange feeling of duty that makes a wife cling to her husband after all good reason for doing so has disappeared. Living with a husband becomes a habit with some women. And as I have said, Bessie was ignorant. It is a fact that all women who laugh easily are usually very naïve; it is the naïve who can afford to laugh heartily.

"One day Kamenetz came to my house and said that he had some important business with me. He saw me often, although when he sat with me he seldom said anything of consequence, and in order to while away the time I would play pinochle with him. This time, after sitting with me for a few minutes with hardly a word, he asked me abruptly:

" 'Do you know Salkind?'

"Of course I knew Salkind. He was the leading juvenile of the company I was with that season.

" 'You are a man I trust, Hyman,' Kamenetz said to me. 'And you will tell me the truth? They say Salkind is paying attentions to Bessie. What they say, I don't mind much, but you tell me. Do you know anything about it?'

"If I had known anything, my answer would have been the same. I don't believe in mixing up in domestic affairs. So I said:

" 'You are foolish to think of it, Kamenetz. Salkind is a handsome young man, and he doesn't need to turn his attention to married women. The fact is, I have never seen him alone with Bessie at any time.'

" 'If you say no, you must know,' Kamenetz said, and with that he left me, as impassive and as gloomy as ever.

"I must confess to you I had paid little attention to Salkind or Bessie. It was not my habit to hang around the coffee-houses, though occasionally I drink a glass of tea at Marcus's. But the idea having been put into my head by Kamenetz, I did take occasion to observe the young people. And I must admit that when I saw them once during a rehearsal standing close together, I felt that Kamenetz had good reason for being jealous.

"Salkind was one of the first of our new recruits; he had youth, good looks, and a certain amount of talent. He had been on the stage for only a few seasons, but he had made a good impression. All our juveniles, till then, were more or less inclined to heaviness of features and weight. That was why Salkind, although a mediocre actor, was able to hold his own for several seasons. He was a handsome chap, with dark eyes and hair, and with broad, erect shoulders.

"And when I saw Bessie near him, her slight figure alert, her mouth ready to smile at the least provocation, I thought it would be one of nature's miscarriages if they did not fall in love with each other.

"I thought very little of the matter, though, until the following season. I spent my vacation, as usual, in the Catskills, with my family. Bessie left for Coney Island, where she boarded with a private family, and Kamenetz, I understood, went out with one of those strolling companies that startle the provinces with their awful contortions during the summer, and usually return to New York via the Tie Line. Salkind spent the summer at Sea Gate, which is not far from Coney Island, for his brother had a cottage there. When Kamenetz returned from his tour, having barely covered his expenses, and more taciturn than ever, he did not join Bessie at Coney Island, but went out there every Sunday.

"It had become evident that there was something between Salkind and Bessie. The young man was taken with her, that was certain, and when the season opened he took no pains to disguise his feelings. Nor did Bessie pretend that the gossips were wrong. She walked about with a strange light in her eyes. She was a little more serious, there was a pathetic droop to her mouth, and she seemed to be more cordial toward Kamenetz in an apologetic way, but in all other respects she was the same genial, vivacious soubrette.

"Kamenetz watched the game from under heavy eyelids. If he did not understand, the wits in the coffee-house made it clear to him. But he did not upbraid her, nor did he quarrel with her. He seemed to be nursing a grievance im-

possible to articulate. He closed himself in, and brooded
over it.

"The thing that hurt him, that made him lose interest in
life, was not the fact that he felt certain that his wife had a
lover. He might have endured that. He had taken chances
when he married a young girl, full of life, when he was
about to go down the second half of his career. He knew
the ways of life, and could not plead ignorance. But when
he saw whom she had selected as a lover, the personification
of everything he was not, the ignominy of it pressed into
his heart and filled him with unutterable fury, fury against
himself, against the offender, against the world. For his rival
deserved the victory! The Yiddish theatre had closed its
doors to Kamenetz. The actors did not relish his company.
He was useless, an irrelevant atom of humanity. Nor did
his family need him. He hardly dared face his children, for
he felt that day by day they were becoming less and less
his. And there stood Salkind, graceful, genial, prosperous,
a rising actor, a popular idol. Had his wife fallen in love
with somebody unknown to the theatre, who had never
entered the circles where he was known, whom his comrades
never met, he might have hidden his shame and never said
anything.

"He brooded over it. Yet he was constantly on guard to
avoid anyone who might attempt to speak to him of his
wife. Whenever he dropped in to see me, he listened to
what I knew of theatre gossip, and never sought to introduce
anything related to Salkind. He pretended that he did not
know, that he was not interested, that he had more important business than to listen to idle rumors.

"One night Kamenetz encountered Salkind in the café.
Kamenetz raised his head from the table and saw his handsome rival. At once his eyes shifted. Salkind strode over to

a center table, pushed back his hat from his forehead, and ordered a small steak.

"But the crowd was in a mood to circulate gossip of interest to Salkind. One of them, a performer in a music-hall, remarked, loud enough for both Kamenetz and Salkind to hear:

" 'Why hasn't Salkind brought Bessie with him?'

" 'He has already taken her home,' her companion observed slyly.

"Salkind greeted this sally with a smile, and assured his friends that Bessie was indisposed or she would have come in with him for a glass of tea.

" 'And what would Kamenetz say,' added the first speaker, 'if he knew about it, eh?'

" 'Kamenetz may say and think what he likes,' said Salkind, with a keen glance in Kamenetz's direction. 'There is nothing he can do about it.'

"I glanced at Kamenetz and was surprised to see the change his features had undergone. His face was usually inexpressive, its color pallid, but now he was flushed, and there was a strange, dangerous glint in his eye, which I had never seen there. His hand trembled, and he arose with an effort from his seat and walked over to Salkind's table. At once all eyes were turned to the group in the center of the room. The light-hearted conversation was hushed, and several women drew their skirts together as if about to leave.

"Kamenetz stood a few moments, held his eye fixed on Salkind, who returned his gaze calmly, and then, with a great effort, as if his tongue refused to lend itself to form the words, he burst out with:

" '*Liebhaber mine*. You are not playing with wooden swords! Take care, I tell you—take care!'

"Salkind stood up and placed his hand upon Kamenetz's shoulder and said, calmly:

" 'If you want to threaten me, come outside.'

"And he took him by the arm and was about to lead him to the door. But before they reached the door Kamenetz wrenched his arm loose, and for some inexplicable reason returned to his seat, moodily, and took up the conversation with his companion. It was as though nothing had happened.

"Salkind shrugged his shoulders, paid for his meal, and left the place. The buzz of conversation was renewed, and the incident seemed to be closed.

"About ten days later I was seated at breakfast—it was close to the noon hour—when the door of my flat was thrown open and in rushed Kamenetz. He startled me. He looked as though he had not slept for weeks. His face was ashen pale, his under lip hung loose, and his eyes were bloodshot. He lurched into a chair, dropped his head on his arm, and burst into a fit of hysterical sobbing. I rushed to him and asked him to tell me what was wrong. I sent my wife into the kitchen, with a caution to be quiet, and then tried to bring him to his senses.

" 'Nothing will help me now,' he cried. 'I am a lost man.'

" 'What has happened, Kamenetz? Why do you sit there like an old woman, crying?' I asked. 'What's wrong?'

"He sobbed for a while, and then he said:

" 'I have killed them both.'

" 'What do you mean?' I cried. 'Whom have you killed? Are you crazy, man?'

" 'I saw him playing with my little boy,' he continued, as if I had not interrupted him. 'I saw him playing with my boy, caressing him, fondling him, and I saw her with her hand on his shoulder, looking at him with love in her eyes. And I felt the ground fall from under me! I could have endured anything! But I thought of my children growing up and forgetting me, loathing me, the only things in the world that mean anything to me also taken away from me. So I killed them both!'

"He said this in a dull manner, as if in a trance, as if the words were formed mechanically, as if he had memorized them, and by hypnotic suggestion they were coming forth from their hiding place in his memory. I shook him.

" 'I killed them!' he repeated. 'They thought I was in Philadelphia. I came in early this morning and found him sitting in my home, taking his breakfast, as if he owned the place, and my children were romping about him, calling him by his first name, I was an unexpected guest, but I was prepared. I waited for the moment when Bessie sent the children out of the room, and when she was alone with him I saw how eager she was to offer herself up to him. From my hiding place I could see how seductive she was, and how he was bound to succumb—he couldn't help himself. So I pulled the trigger, once, twice, I don't know how many times, and I saw both of them fall. I ran from the place, my ears ringing with their cries. I have done it! It has been burning in my heart for months. I have suffered hell fire. I have been in a living death. Now it is all over! I feel quiet again.'

" 'Do you think you are going to escape punishment?' I cried. 'Do you imagine I am going to harbor a wretch like you? What right have you to kill them? You had no right to marry a girl like Bessie from the start. You'll have to get right out of here! Get out, you murderer, you murderer!' And I opened the door for him, filled with rage.

"When he heard me call him what he was, he broke out into whimpering, and implored me not to turn him out, and what he said was so insanely childish that I though he might be mistaken about the whole affair, that he had not actually committed a double murder, that he might have gone crazy brooding over his troubles, and in an insane moment dreamed that he had killed them.

"I drew him back into the room, and pushed him into the hall bedroom, locking the door behind him. Then I went into the kitchen and told my wife to keep an eye on Kamenetz, that he was asleep, but a bit delirious, and that she shouldn't mind anything she might hear from him. My wife was troubled, but I told her not to be alarmed.

"I walked rapidly toward 12th Street, where Bessie lived, and as I walked my mind was filled with apprehension. I consoled myself with the thought that, after all, Kamenetz might have been mistaken.

"When I arrived at 12th Street I saw a throng in front of the apartment house, and several policeman patrolling the block. An ambulance was drawn up before the house. After a great deal of trouble, I persuaded the police to let me pass through. I entered the house and soon had a chance to see the tragic results of Kamenetz's morning work. Bessie lay on the couch, her garments undone, bleeding, and a doctor was working at her side. On a chair sat Salkind, pale, his arm bandaged. He walked about nervously, watching the doctor at his task, and groaning. I heard the cries of children in the next room.

"I turned to the doctor and asked: 'Is it anything serious?' Bessie opened her eyes and saw me. She seemed to recognize me, but she could not speak.

"'There certainly is hope,' said the doctor, cautiously, 'but it all depends upon her will to live.' He continued his work. Salkind turned his face to the wall and wept.

"I said to Salkind: 'Don't trouble about the children. I will take them with me.'

"I went into the next room and took the two children and brought them over to my cousin's who lived on the same block, and then I ran back home. I was met on the stairs by my wife, who was almost hysterical with fear.

" 'There is something wrong with Kamenetz,' she exclaimed.

"I unlocked the door where I had placed Kamenetz. There lay the murderer, prone on his face, dead, with a revolver in his hand.

"Left alone, his fears destroyed him. Perhaps he had thought of the future of his children, perhaps he had balanced his accounts with the world and found that he ought to pay what he owed it by dying. He was buried the same day from my house.

"Since then La Belle Kamenetz, as you call her, is in retirement. She did not die, nor did she fully recover. She suffers pains in her limbs. She cannot sing or dance. To my mind, she is more beautiful today than she ever was, but it is not the sort of beauty that shows up well on the stage. It is too pensive, there are too many lines, it doesn't lend itself to soubrette work. Perhaps, after a few more years she may be more than a soubrette, you can't tell. Experience has given her character. And she has her children.

"Salkind? Oh, of course Salkind married Bessie, and you would be astonished to see the devotion of that fellow. He is a much better actor than he was then. His life is spent in serving Bessie. He is an exceptional husband. That is the finest thing that has come out of that prosaic, wretched tragedy. They had been tried together in the furnace of a bitter common experience.

"You would be interested to know that Kamenetz's boy has taken to the violin, and people say that he has talent. It was Salkind who discovered his talent. He is just as proud

of little Max Kamenetz as Kamenetz himself might have
been had he not attempted to break the triangle. For, after
all, what real difference did it make to Kamenetz—the existence of that affair? He should have closed his eyes to it;
but there is a perversity about jealousy it is hard to explain."

VIII

A Lesson in Matrimony

KURASH WAS A STOCKY YOUNG MAN WHO, BY SHEER PERSIST-
ence, had forced himself into the Yiddish theatre as an actor.
He knew how to read Yiddish, but had never gone to any
school. He thought he was reaching high when he aspired to
be an actor, and when he finally got his opportunity, he was
satisfied with small parts. He served his apprenticeship in a
music-hall. His picture always appeared on the posters in
the last row, when it appeard at all. When he was taken
into the union, his ambition rested.

He was reticent and obstinate in a mild way. He had few
intimate friends, and no one in the theatre knew much of
the life he led when he left the theatre. If he had any interests or pleasures, they were kept away from the flow of
gossip that enlivened the coffee-houses. In appearance he
suggested a workman in a sweatshop. He boarded with a
family on Second Avenue, who seldom saw him.

And yet, beneath his reticence, he was restless. He often

strolled in the vicinity of 23rd Street in a shame-faced manner, seeking to find among the liberated and carefree denizens of that quarter some response to the turbulent desires that agitated him. It was to be had for money; he knew of no art that would evoke it otherwise. The bright lights of Broadway allured him, and he loitered about the famous street quite alone, head down and eyes filled with curiosity.

One night he left the theatre after the second act, in which he had a small part, took a car to 42nd Street, and slowly walked down Sixth Avenue, turning up 34th Street, until he reached Fourth Avenue, and halted at Union Square. He sat down on one of the benches. Before him through the skeleton trees—it was still April—he saw the massive, moving lights of the Keith Theatre, and cars rushing back and forth like fireflies. Crowds of people passed him, rushing home for supper; others, by their careless manner, their indolent puffing of cigarettes, their shifting glances, gave evidence of a carefree desire to meet those accidents of pseudo-romance in quest of which Kurash himself had come to that quarter.

As he sat there in comparative darkness, confronted by the blaze of light and flanked on both sides by the riff-raff of the great metropolis, hearing subdued murmurs from them, he felt so sympathetic toward the whole world that he unbuttoned his heavy overcoat, which he had not yet discarded, and lit another cigarette. The match flared and lit up his features. He then leaned back to enjoy his smoke.

A shadow passed him, hesitated, and turned back. He heard the swish of skirts, and then felt, for he did not look up, the soft warmth of a presence beside him. He heard her regular breathing, but he dared not look up. Then he heard her voice. He raised his eyes.

"It is a nice evening, isn't it?" she said.

Kurash saw before him a plump little girl, with dark hair and flashing eyes, in which he discerned instinctively (and with apprehension) a racial affinity to himself.

"You are a Jewess," he said sorrowfully.

"You needn't look so glum about it," the girl laughed, as she came a little closer.

"Whenever I see a girl like you, walking the street, and find she is a Jewish girl," said Kurash, "I feel—I can't describe it to you—as if I had met my own sister on the street."

"You're a strange fellow," said the girl. "Will you walk?"

So Kurash walked with her. She prattled as they walked, and told him, in a strangely naïve manner, all about herself. He interrupted with many laconic questions, and so they passed away into the night.

He met her again and they went to the theatre together. She told him her story in greater detail, and he felt sorry for her. She had no relatives, no friends, and had taken to the street after several years of domestic service with hard mistresses. Kurash noticed that she was well dressed, that she had a certain talent in telling a story, and that she was also anxious to know something of his life. He told her what there was to tell, and when she learned that he was an actor her eyes opened wide and she wanted to know whether he knew certain actors, whose names she gave with a note of familiarity.

After a little urging she consented to let Kurash visit her in her room.

"Why do you wish to visit me?" she asked.

"Out here in the street, or at the theatre," he replied, "one can't feel as much at home."

"You can come," she finally said.

The house she lived in was leased by a middle-aged woman with a sour face, who seemed to know that her lodger was not all she should be, but who, at the same time, did not scruple to profit by the extra rental this class of women paid her. She had her breakfasts in the house, but all other meals she ate in a restaurant around the corner.

Kurash felt diffident the first time he entered her room. He was ill at ease; he was a bit afraid, but there was something so fresh in Hannah's appearance, and so cordial in her manner, that he felt as if he were visiting a girl with whom he had spent his childhood.

He came to her one night and, after a good deal of hesitation, told her of a plan. He had given the matter much thought. He felt certain that it would take her out of her present way of life. She listened to him intently, seated on her trunk He moved from the one chair in the room to the bed, and leaned over its back to get a better look at her.

"Well, what do you propose?" asker the girl, adjusting her hair.

"I have thought the matter over very carefully," he said. "A girl like you ought not to be in this business. There is one way out of it."

Hannah leaned forward and held the back of his head with her palm. Her lips protuded as if she were about to kiss him.

"If you know a way that isn't hard," she said, still smiling.

"You know me now for three weeks," said Kurash. "I am a man without relatives. I have worked myself up from being a common workman to the position of an actor. I get a fairly good salary. I have no responsibilities. Since I first met you, I don't know why, but your image is always with me. Maybe because you, too, are all alone. Maybe because you come from the same part of Russia that I do; but, at any rate, I like you, and if you will have me, I should be very glad to marry you."

Hannah arose and turned her face to the wall, touching lightly a curtain that hid her assortment of dresses.

"You don't mean it!" she murmured.

"I have thought the matter over very carefully," he repeated. "I have never met a girl who inspired me with such good feelings. I am no prude, as you know. I have gone through the whirlwind of passion which most men pass through. With most men it scars them; with others it leaves them indifferent to good feelings. With me it has left a certain sadness. That's why I say, marry me, and I'll try to make you happy."

She turned to him and fell weeping against his shoulder. He asked her why she wept.

"It's because you offer me something I'm afraid of," she said. "You don't know what this life makes of a girl. There must be something in me that made it possible for me to do what I have done. I don't know what to do!"

Kurash tried to comfort her.

"All your fears are baseless. You are different," he said. "You will be marrying one who knows all about you. You haven't been changed much. You will look back upon your life until now as if it belonged to another girl."

She stood up, tears brimming her eyes, and raised his face to hers. She looked at him intently for a few moments and then said:

"It is agreed!" said Kurash. He was confident of himself.

"I agree, but upon one condition: whatever may happen between us you will never reproach me for what has been. If your faith in me is lost, you will let me go without regret!"

They were married, and for several weeks lived in seclusion. Kurash furnished a flat, and found that his young wife was a good cook. He showered her with attentions, and gave her a number of small luxuries that quite overcame her.

Kurash was elated. He told none of his fellow actors, and anticipated the surprised remarks of all his friends when he should present his wife. He felt in unusually good health, and lost the gravity of his demeanor, the stiffness which had always been characteristic of his acting.

"Where would you like to go tonight, my dear?" said Kurash, coming into the flat about six o'clock.

"Let's go to the Yiddish theatre, and after the show to Marcus's," she said.

A large number of Yiddish actors were gathered in Marcus's that night. They looked up when Kurash entered with a pretty young woman at his heels. They winked and, hailing Kurash with generous familiarity, forced him to introduce the young woman. The word was passed about the café, and Kurash was at once the recipient of congratulations. Hannah met their advances with a vivacious smile, and in a little while she and Kurash were seated with a group of players, buzzing with conversation.

Kurash was disturbed. He had never seen Hannah so vivacious. She seemed to be eager to make a good impression, and by a strange coincidence those about her, except for the wife of Gold, were all men, and they seemed to be enjoying her bright sallies. He noticed that the women instinctively stood aloof, and he felt hurt. He went over to their group and invited them over to be introduced to his wife, and from the manner they accepted the invitation he felt that feminine intuition in some subtle way made them unappreciative of the honor. Just then he heard a merry peal of laughter from Hannah.

That night he was reticent, while his wife prattled of the good time she had had. He fell into a restless sleep. He looked at the figure beside him and marveled at her indifference to the contempt of other women.

Within a short space of time Hannah became quite well

known to the acting fraternity. She would wait for her husband in the evenings, and before going home they stepped into the café for tea. Kurash was soon accustomed to the strange glances thrown in his direction whenever he appeared with his wife. She seemed just as pretty as before—she was just as interesting—but the glamor of the relation had begun to fade. He could not describe the difference in the impression her conduct now made upon him. All his relations with women had been with those whom he encountered and passed, never to meet again. He regarded them as in a class by themselves. But now he saw in his wife a strange, inordinate desire for unusual sensations, the fever of sport, and an indifference to his presence in the private, personal things of life that made him feel ill at ease.

But he became more affectionate, more tender, like a mother. And Hannah seemed to notice a change in him, too, but the displeasing things that set him on edge were beyond her control; she obeyed the impulse, and regretted it afterward.

One night he left the theatre earlier than he had anticipated. As he emerged he saw his wife in conversation with a man whose back was turned. Hannah was unaware of his approach, and when he called to her she turned and hurriedly introduced the man, whom Kurash knew as one of the attendants in the theatre across the street. He greeted the man pleasantly, and passed on with his wife.

"What were you doing here, Hannah?" he asked softly.

"I came to meet you," she replied, and then, noting the set expression on his face, she added: "He is an old friend."

Kurash bit his lips and they walked on in silence. When they arrived at Grand Street she paused, as if to turn the corner.

"Let's not go to the café tonight," he said.

Then began Kurash's martyrdom. He felt irritated that Hannah did not offer any explanation. He was annoyed at her silence. He did not find the same pleasure in his home life as before. He wanted to berate her, to demand her confidence, but he lacked the courage. He stayed away from home on the evenings when he was not employed. He wandered about the quarter with a desire to speak frankly to her, but he never could bring himself to the point of asking what she was thinking of. He was afraid of her reply.

He sought to stifle his suspicions. Once he imagined he saw her in Union Square, the same brown skirt and the same hat on her head, the same furtive glancing about. He imagined her a vampire, prowling about the streets, seeking someone to devour, and on such evenings when he returned home he was ashamed to look at her. He would find her in bed, sleeping soundly, breathing regularly, with a smile about her lips. She always looked very virginal when he came upon her asleep in bed.

She was as affectionate and devoted as ever, it appeared to Kurash. She was a scrupulously clean housekeeper and attentive to all household duties, but she made no effort to introduce domestic warmth in the house, which the natural woman brings with her almost anywhere, whether in a hotel room, in a flat or a tenement, or in a mansion. Everything was carefully arranged, but something was lacking.

"You don't take me to Marcus's as you used to," she said to him once.

"Marcus's is no place for you," he replied harshly.

She stood as if transfixed, deliberated a moment, started to speak, but then turned and left the room.

He tried to reason himself out of his dilemma, but constantly there arose before him the picture of his wife speaking so confidently, in so comradely a way, with the man in front of the theatre, and her remark that she had known him "from before." Her past was a fathomless pit—he dared not look down into it. Why was he worried? It was because he saw the past reflected in her eyes.

He wondered how many men there were walking the streets of New York who had known her "from before," how many heads were turned when he and Hannah walked together. He was frightened at the thought. His home was polluted every time he thought of that army of men. He was coupled to a being who might, at a moment's notice, be coupled with any of dozens of other men.

He played his parts in the theatre with an intensity which caused comment. He was conscious of improvement in his acting, but felt no interest in it. Toward the end of the season the resident companies went on tour. They always returned for the weekend performances, which still drew paying houses. Kurash went with his company several times and left his wife at home. At first he had thought of taking Hannah with him, then, because she pleaded indisposition and pointed to the extra cost, he thought it better to go alone. Besides, to take her with him would have created gossip, for none of the actors took their wives with them on tour.

On a Tuesday evening the company arrived in Baltimore. They played that night, and were to play the following night also. At one o'clock on Wednesday a telegram arrived asking that Kurash be sent back to New York in order to fill out a special cast, which was to give a performance that night. Kurash took the first train and arrived in New York in time to take a bite and appear in the first act. After the performance he left the theatre, intending to go home.

He hesitated and decided to spend a few minutes in the café. As he was about to enter Marcus's he saw through the window the form of his wife; opposite her sat a player who was well known to him. Kurash started, but did not enter.

He waited in a doorway. They soon passed him and he followed them, turning his coat collar up and pulling his hat over his eyes. They walked along, chatting with animation. He saw them halt before his home, and then the man went up with Hannah and left Kurash standing on the opposite side of the street, stunned. He stood there for fully fifteen minutes. Then he entered the first saloon he saw and drank a great deal of liquor. How he happened to be in the hotel where he found himself the next morning, he never knew.

He thought calmly of the whole affair and reasoned with himself. He felt that to return to Hannah was well-nigh impossible. He knew her now, and there was no further need of considering the matter. He went up to his flat the following day and found Hannah at home, expecting him. He spoke to her now without any effort to disguise the fact that he considered her a stranger. Something had happened that effaced all they had in common—he saw nothing but a blank when he looked sternly into her eyes.

He greeted her coldly, and passed into the bedroom, returning with a suitcase.

"Where are you going?" she asked.

"I am leaving you," he said, his eyes lowered.

"No!" she said skeptically.

"Yes," he replied.

"What's the matter?" she asked, coming closer to him. He thrust her to one side.

"You know well enough," he said. "You have deceived me. I thought marrying you would make a good woman of you, but I see that I was wrong. You are bad, and you can't change. It isn't in you."

"What have I done?" she asked, suddenly becoming brazen.

"You are one of those women, Hannah," he said, "who can't remain loyal to one man. One man is not enough for you, one home is not enough for you, one love is not enough for you. You are bound to go to the dogs."

And as he said this he saw that Hannah had thrown off the mask of naïveté, that she now had the face of the hardened woman, and he became enraged.

"Why do you stand there like that?" he shouted. "Why don't you say something? Why are you dumb?"

The girl sat down on the bed, rubbed her eyes, which were filling with tears, and then stammered a reply:

"A man can't understand this, so I can't explain to you. You are right. I am different from other women. I can't remain true to one man; all men attract me. I want them; I can't help it! I don't ask loyalty of you—have never asked it. So why should you ask it of me? What I am not, I cannot be!"

"You are a harlot," said Kurash. "But to hell with that! Everything I could have forgiven, but to bring men into this home, to lend yourself to all sorts of indignities here. You are not a woman, you are a shameless prostitute!"

She buried her face in the pillow and murmured: "That is what I am! That is what I have become."

Kurash left her there, her hair disheveled, her blouse unbuttoned, crying bitterly with her hands covering her face. She did not move as he slammed the door. He had known harlots, but had never been affected by them. But he now felt that something unclean had gotten into his blood.

He never saw her again. Nor could he bear to meet his fellow players in the theatre. He left New York, giving no address. Years later it was reported that he had become a prosperous shop-keeper in Texas, but the Yiddish theatre never saw him again. They say he joined a synagogue, and acquired a reputation for piety.

IX

His First Hit

THE FIRST DICTATOR IN THE YIDDISH THEATRE WAS GOLDFADEN, and for a time his rule was unchallenged. Not only was he the manager, but he owned a repertoire of successful plays which he had written, and in which his own music was an essential part. His actors did not fight for their rights; they deserted and fled to other communities, where they set up rickety theatres of their own. They left him alone in the ruins of his empire. Years later, when Goldfaden came to New York, penniless, he spoke of himself as King Lear, the victim of the ingratitude of his children, the actors.

The second tyrant was the actor-manager. That was inevitable. One actor always had to be in the lead. Plays were written after the pattern of life, and life also creates its stars. That one actor should have his name on the posters in red letters if he played the leading part was unavoidable. He was more important than the supporting cast. Disputes between the players often served to boost the better player

129

ahead of his rival. As the theatre grew in importance, a lease became a costly investment. When the question arose in whose name the lease should be taken, it became necessary that an "angel" appear, who could be persuaded to take a peculiar interest in the star player—usually an actress. The lease was negotiated in the name of the angel whose golden wings protected the star. The angel would have his wings clipped in short order when he had served the purpose of his life, and then the star shone in all his glory, alone, and became inevitably both the leading player and the manager; in other words, the star-manager.

With the advent of the star-manager the union was born —to recover for the actors some part of the heritage they had lost. The whole theatre was unionized—from actors to ushers. The actors' union found it necessary to limit the number of its members and to maintain a front of antagonism against every aspirant for the stage. It was a guild. It wanted to keep its monopoly. It raised the initiation fee beyond the means of the amateur. It forced applicants to pass the hurdle of examinations which were designed to obstruct and prevent admission. The examiners were chosen for their hardness of heart. Many a tale was told of the ingenuity of the examiners who discouraged the young hopefuls and kept them on the waiting list for years. The door of the theatre opened only when it was forced.

Krantz wanted to be a Yiddish actor. He was young and quick in mimicry. He was in love with Yiddish, and being good to look at he thought of himself as a declaimer and then as an impersonator. He joined an amateur dramatic club, and was admired and praised by the intelligentsia. When he confided his ambition to his orthodox father there was a row, which ended with Krantz running away from home. He took passage on a cattleboat for London.

There he found the dregs of a troupe that was scarcely able
to keep body and soul together. He played for a season and
emerged in the spring like a starved wolf after a bad winter.
He decided to leave the fogs of London, and joined a number of his comrades in a tour of South Africa. The diamond
mines had made Johannesburg a boom town. There Krantz
played for two years and got experience. He became an
expert in sticking long beards on his handsome face. But
after a while he wanted to get back home and show his own
people what had become of him. He arranged a benefit
performance and earned enough money to buy his passage
back to New York.

But the actors' union refused to recognize him. He showed
them photographs and clippings he had accumulated in
Johannesburg, but all this evidence left them cold. They
looked at Krantz with frigid, fishy eyes. They were adamant.

"But I've just come from Johannesburg," said Krantz,
"and I played there for two seasons. You can see for yourself."

"Don't tell us of Johannesburg," the chairman said. "You
might as well say China. We play in New York."

"But how can I get experience here if I have to be a
union man first?" Krantz yelled.

"That's your own business," said the chairman, and turned
his back.

He was told of a company playing in Philadelphia, with
Dikman as its star. They had a strike on their hands. Krantz
went over there, lingered about the lobby, and followed
Dikman to his favorite restaurant. While Dikman was gorging his meal, Krantz spread his press notices before the fat
actor, who looked at them with suspicion. But Dikman
needed actors, for he wanted to show the union that they
could not intimidate him. Within a few days Krantz found

himself in the company, and was able to play for three
weeks. He thought this amount of experience would suffice
for the record. He returned to union headquarters in New
York, and told the committee that now he was eligible for
membership. He had his Philadelphia record. At first they
laughed, and then turned angry.

"What do you think, you *yold*? Have we fallen so low
that we'll take a self-confessed 'scab' into our union?" shouted
the chairman.

Krantz lost his temper, pushed the chairman back into
his chair, slammed the door behind him, and went out on
the street with murder in his heart. He rushed to the office
of "The Forwards," and told the editor that he was the
victim of a conspiracy. He spoke so well that Kahn wrote
a furious article about the tyranny of unions, who impaired
the solidarity of the proletariat by using monopolistic methods, turning labor organizations into exclusive clubs. Krantz
persuaded Manewitz that the future of the Yiddish theatre
depended upon young talent. What would become of the
theatre if the older men and women prevented the infusion
of new blood? Manewitz sent letters to the leaders of the
union, but nothing happened. Krantz went so far as to
lodge a complaint against the union in the district attorney's
office; the district attorney had the union leaders summoned
to see him, and gave them good legal advice. Upon that
advice the union acted. They ordered the board of examiners
to give Krantz a hearing. A report was filed, and after being
duly examined, the committee found Krantz unfit to be an
actor. They suggested he continue his studies, and said they
would give him another hearing after six months.

Krantz went every day to the coffee-houses frequented by
the Yiddish actors. They listened to him with good humor.
He mocked and abused them. They shrugged their shoul-

ders. Let him talk his heart out, it won't get him into the
union, they said. But one season a number of new companies were organized in the provinces, and there was a
shortage of actors in New York. Without examination, without the payment of an initiation fee, Krantz found himself
a member of Burlak's company. The union had insisted that
Burlak take an additional actor and pay him the minimum
wages. They would not let Burlak get away with one actor
less than the rules prescribed. So they decided to let Krantz
become a union man.

Krantz found that being in the company did not mean a
chance to act. He was an extra, one step removed from the
chorus. He played a servant, with two words to utter. He
was one of a crowd, yelling at the top of his voice as its
leader. He had to play a messenger, but he delivered a mes-
sage in a latter. He always had to use some sort of hairy
disguise. He recorded the year as a total loss.

The second season found him shifted—by sheer accident
—to Ritter's company. Ritter was always irritated by Krantz.
Perhaps his youth offended him, or the superior airs Krantz
put on as defense armor. Ritter resented young blood, its
arrogance, its disdain of the past. But what must have moved
him most was the feeling that as Krantz moved forward,
his own importance would diminish. Ritter felt that Krantz
always looked at him, seeming to say, What is that old
codger doing here so long?

For the time being, however, Krantz's reflections did not
help him. He made no progress in the affections of Ritter.
He received his wages with mounting disgust. He tried to
get Manewitz to intervene, but the dramatist had no appetite for the personal intrigues of the theatre. He wrote a
polite letter to Ritter, mentioning young Krantz, but Ritter
pretended he had not seen it. Then came Ritter's historic

break with Manewitz—a lawsuit, the question of royalties, hot insults exchanged—and this gave Krantz his first real opportunity.

To vent his rage against Manewitz, Ritter decided, since he was forced to produce the latter's newest play, "The True Power," to show Manewitz what he could do with it. He did not intend to be bound by the text or the author's stage directions. He could cut it to suit his own notions. He would show that Cossack how successful plays were made.

The play dealt with a middle-aged doctor whose wife dies and leaves him with a young child, and who decides to marry a fresh young country girl. The doctor has a younger brother who fascinates the young wife, but the husband is so absorbed in his practice that he does not see what is going on. The doctor returns from a typhoid case and learns how his wife has wronged him. In his excitement and indignation he neglects to disinfect himself, and in fondling his own child he infects her with the disease. The child dies, and the husband and wife are reconciled at her deathbed.

In the course of the play, two minor characters come in— one the doctor's assistant, a self-taught village leech, whose stupidity is a source of humor, and the other a Russian student who is the young girl's teacher. The student is a revolutionist, on intimate terms with the doctor, who is shown to be a supporter of the propaganda of the revolutionists.

All the parts were distributed by Ritter except that of the student. Krantz was given no part at all. But the actors who might have played the student all, for various reasons, refused to take it. One was a tenor; the other had "starred" in the provinces. They had the right, under union rules, to refuse to play such a small part or a part not in their special line.

"Look here, you scoundrel," said Ritter to Ginsberg, the tenor, with tears in his eyes. "This part is actually built for you. You have never played a student before. Am I to blame if that Manewitz gave him so few words? You can make up to look handsome. What more do you want?"

But Ginsberg smiled and walked aside.

"If you don't play it, whom have I got?" shouted Ritter.

"It's a part just made for Krantz," said Ginsberg.

"That sham of an actor will have to eat dirt before I let him play in a new production," said Ritter.

Krantz strutted about the stage, unconcerned, and spoke to a friend loud enough for the others to hear.

"I'm the luckiest fellow," he said. "What have I to complain of? He pays me my salary. I don't have much to do, that's true. But let him give me the beards and keep the parts. What difference does that make?"

"What's that?" shouted Ritter. "You don't care if you don't earn your salary?"

"If you don't care, why should I?" said Krantz. "What you pay me is for what you let me do. I might even like to play all your parts and let you have a rest. But you won't let me. I'm ready to work. You think I shouldn't work too hard, so you give me the smallest parts you have. You're the boss. Nothing for me to do—that's your funeral."

"We'll see about that," muttered Ritter. He fingered the manuscript, extracted a few sheets, and handed them to Krantz.

"There's your part," he said. "Like it or not, you are going to play it, and if I see you are no actor, which I have seen before, I'll take this up with the union, so help me God. If for no other reason, I hope this play goes on all season so that you will have to quit playing pinochle and come to the theatre."

The company burst into laughter.

"There's your chance, Krantz," said Mrs. Ritter. "The audience will see your face, and you have nothing to be ashamed of." She liked to have young actors about her. They made her feel warm.

When Krantz got home he read the part eagerly. There were only three scenes in which he appeared. But he was often left standing without speech. In the last act, all his playing consisted of wringing of the hands when the little daughter died.

"It's true, there isn't a beard in this part," he said to his wife that night, "but it's just as short on words as all the others."

"Don't you care," she said. "When you get the part that suits you, you'll turn the tables on them."

"I suppose I'll have a long beard of my own by then," he said gloomily.

In order to feel his way he approached Ritter the next day and said, in a good-natured way:

"This part isn't for me, Mr. Ritter. You can see that for yourself. Take my word for it, it's intended for a much better actor. There are more than three words in it, and three words are my limit."

"Even if the part hasn't one word," Ritter said, "you will have to play it. I have made up my mind to give you your final examination. Either this makes you an actor, or you quit."

The rehearsal was a tedious affair for Krantz. "The True Power" was expanded, condensed, revised, and refined to suit Ritter's whimsical and erratic ideas. In the wrangling at the rehearsal, Krantz was almost forgotten. Whenever he appeared, Ritter's wrath was at once aroused. There were threats that the part might be cut out altogether.

"Now, look here, Krantz," said Ritter, with the perspiration pouring from him. "This part is a straight part. Chayutin is a Russian student. He is not an interfering person. What goes on in the house does not bother him. He acts like a gentleman. So, for God's sake, be a gentleman at least while you are on the stage."

When Krantz left the theatre for home that afternoon, he felt that nothing could stave off a final break with Ritter. It was impossible for him to play Chayutin as Ritter wanted him to play it.

He walked through Grand Street. The day was dark and soggy. The sidewalks were deep in liquid mud, and on the backs of the coats of men hurrying through the street there were thin streaks of slush. Krantz paused before a store where dress suits were rented, and glanced at the puppet in the window togged out in white cotton gloves, high hat, and cutaway coat. When he saw that figure a sudden idea struck him. The faint image of the character of Chayutin, which had been hovering in his thoughts for many days, came to life.

That night he invested in an old slouch hat, a tight-fitting standing collar, a four-in-hand tie so stiff that it couldn't be kept from crawling up his collar, a pair of trousers that looked like a bag, and an old raincoat with short sleeves that had a mantle and did not fit around the neck.

When he next appeared at rehearsals he was as meek as a lamb. He listened to Mrs. Ritter's silly advice with great respect. When Ritter told him to efface himself in the third act, to hide somewhere in a corner, he got off the stage with a laugh.

The East Side was keyed up to a high pitch in advance of the first night's performance. Accounts of a law suit with Manewitz, carefully edited puffs of Ritter and Mrs. Ritter,

interviews with the great actor, appeared in the Yiddish
papers. "The True Power" was a realistic, high-class, literary
play. Naturally, a large audience of curious people appeared
on the evening of the first performance.

Krantz arrived early and went to his dressing-room. When
the callboy yelled for Krantz, he brought him into his room
and cautioned him not to let anybody come in to see him.
He locked the door before he turned to his make-up box.

Ritter was in the midst of a scene with his prospective
father-in-law and mother-in-law when Krantz entered as
Chayutin. It was his business to turn and greet Chayutin,
but Ritter stood stock still, as though petrified. He thought
that a tramp wandering in the back-stage alley had lost his
way and stumbled upon the stage. He saw before him a
weak-chested and near-sighted man who was dressed in a
raincoat, over which a mantle was flung; it was dripping
wet, shabby and torn, with short sleeves. On the back of
his head was an old slouch hat. His trousers were short,
and he wore a high collar with a tie struggling upward. A
little mustache decorated his face. He stood there, peering
curiously at Ritter. This was not the student he was expecting. When the prompter again motioned to him to
shake hands with the newcomer, Ritter did so indifferently,
while a burst of applause broke from the audience. By this
time he saw through Krantz's disguise and muttered to the
prompter seated in his box:

"What does this mean?"

The audience had recognized Chayutin. Ritter might
think that he was no Russian student, but they knew the
type better. They recognized without any hesitation the
blundering, slovenly, near-sighted individual with books
under his arm as the prototype of hundreds of such persons
on the East Side.

Ritter went through the scene without a murmur, but when he had a few moments of silence, he said to Krantz, in an aside, with a touch of pathos in his voice:

"You saboteur! Haven't I told you Chayutin is a gentleman? Have you ever seen a student rigged up as you are? This is terrible. I'll sack you after the performance if it's the last thing I do."

"Excuse me, Mr. Ritter," said Krantz, also in an aside. "If you don't like this make-up, I can change it in the next act. It makes no difference to me."

Their conversation was interrupted, but when Ritter resumed with Krantz, he said in the same subdued, pathetic voice:

"Are you crazy? How can you come in the second act in different make-up? That is impossible. You play the rest of the evening as you are. I'll have it out with you later."

Ritter then took the center of the stage, and in a few minutes the act was over.

When the curtain fell, the applause was deafening. Ritter had really distinguished himself and was prepared to take a curtain call. He was so overcome by the cheers that he took his wife's hand and stepped before the footlights with a humble bow. This performance was repeated four times. But then there came a shout which grew in strength and finally was distinguished as:

"Chayutin! Chayutin!"

Between bows, Ritter murmured to his wife:

"Who's this Chayutin?"

"They must mean Krantz," said his wife.

Ritter left the stage in disgust, but the cries for Chayutin continued until the orchestra drowned out their voices.

Although Ritter pretended he had no respect for his audience, he was always influenced by public opinion. He never pitted his theoretical knowledge against the opinions of his audience. He believed, as a matter of principle, that the audience was right, although privately he inveighed against them. He decided not to have it out with Krantz after the first act.

In the second act, as he came upon the stage, Krantz felt that he had made an impression upon the audience, which audibly gave signs of recognition. They seemed to know him —and that had never happened to him before. He was lifted up by the invisible transmission of influence which gives life to the player. He redoubled his efforts and forgot that dismissal faced him, feeling only that he must make the most of his opportunity. Encouraged by the audience, he introduced many details of stage business which filled out the sketch of the character he had merely projected in the first act.

Ritter did not have it out with Krantz after the second act.

In the third act, Ritter was under the influence of his own part and paid no attention to Krantz. He played his own role with intensity and vigor, which carried the house, and inasmuch as Krantz took part in those scenes, Ritter for the first time felt that the silent, intense and intelligent byplay of Krantz gave him an effective support. For the first time Krantz lived in his role and gave all his intelligence to the proper modulation of his part of the dialogue. It was in this act that Chayutin had a scene in which, after having received many favors from Goldenweiser (Ritter), he must speak out frankly and denounce the great physician for his blundering behavior toward his wife. This was Chayutin's longest speech—though it really was not long at all—but Krantz did it with such sincerity and at the same time so softly that Ritter himself was affected, and when Krantz was recalled he felt that the young man had earned the applause. He was amazed to feel that Krantz had moved him, an experienced player, with just a few words of declamation.

It was after twelve when the curtain fell on the last act. The audience clamored for all the actors. They did not desist until the young actor appeared before them minus his little mustache, his goggles and his faded coat. Krantz was timid and nervous and would have run away. He looked anxiously at Ritter, who went over to him and took his hand, and the four actors appeared before the curtain.

Krantz looked squarely at an audience for the first time in his life. For the first time he realized that he had established contact with the people on the other side of the lights. He knew now what it meant to be an actor. He did not care what happened to him after that experience.

He was still in his dressing-room when Ritter appeared at the door, dressed for the street. Krantz looked anxiously at him, wiped his face with a towel, and felt nervous under his gaze. The great actor held out his hand and said:

"Your pardon, Krantz. It was I who was mistaken. You may never have been an actor. You certainly waste your time playing cards, for tonight's performance shows you to be an artist, and I am proud of you!"

Krantz arose and with his make-up towel still in his hand, saluted, and said:

"After seeing you play tonight, Mr. Ritter, I am glad to say that I am proud to be praised by an artist like you."

That was that. It sounded good. It made Krantz feel good. His wife that night felt good. It was the beginning of his career. He had made a hit.

But what passed between him and Ritter was only for the moment. It was a passing emotion that faded away and could not be renewed in the days that followed. Ritter was a man of temperament. Within a month, the part of Chayutin was reduced to a shadow. Every evening saw a piece taken out of it. Ritter pushed the part out of every scene, reduced the text, and before the season was over, though Krantz could boast that at last he was playing without a beard, the beardless part was definitely in the background.

X

The Phoenix

IN HER FAR PAST MME. RACHEL HAD BEEN A POOR, FRIENDLESS working girl, caught in the turmoil of the East Side. Her only relative was a peevish old aunt. She did not know the way out of the Ghetto in which she had been brought up. Life was a monotonous drudgery, the horizon gray and the future as drab as the present.

Her aunt was submerged in the mean pursuits of life, with an incompetent husband on her hands and three or four young children. At the factory where Rachel worked she was one of many hands mechanically performing tasks placed before them. They turned up every morning, robots awakened by an invisible master's alarm clock. Rachel often wondered what all these "hands" did between whiles, how they spent their evenings, whether they were all as restless and as ignorant as she.

For months she had observed in the workroom, not far from her, a young girl with a bright face, piercing eyes, and

jet-black hair, who sat almost doubled up at her work. The
girl had a curved spine, but her misfortune, instead of sour-
ing her temper, seemed to have had the opposite effect. Now,
instead of singing vaudeville songs, in broken English, the
shop heard coming from the throat of Liza the songs of
their own people, Yiddish melodies, sweet and pathetic, some
of them with a merry swing, many of them grave and sad. It
was Liza who brought the muse of Jewish song into the
barren shop. When Rachel heard these songs she felt the
unrest of youth more clearly expressed than it had been in
her dreams.

Between Liza and Rachel—the one deformed but merry,
the other beautiful but discontented and moody—a friendship grew up.

When they became friends Rachel asked Liza:

"Where do you get the Yiddish songs you sing? I never
heard them before."

"Where have you been, then?" inquired Liza, laughing.
"Don't you know that the East Side is full of songs, sad and
gay, all grown here, springing out of the life of our people?"

"I guessed as much," said Rachel, "but where do they
come from?"

Rachel had never known her mother's voice, had no like-
ness of her to recall the features of the woman who had
given life to her, and who must have sung to her lovingly
during the four or five months she lived after her daughter
was born. There were no cradle songs in Rachel's memory.

"Come with me, I'll show you where they make the Jewish
songs," said Liza.

She took Rachel to the Yiddish theatre, where they saw
one of Lecker's absurd operettas. But the girls did not mind
Lecker's operetta, for they heard the music. It was not original; it was not sung well; and the words were utterly mean-

ingless; but it was Jewish music. It did not matter who had written it. It seemed as though the tunes had come up out of the Jewish soil like oil rising to the surface.

Rachel felt as though a burden had been lifted from her heart. The echo of songs rang in her ears for weeks, and she renewed the echo at the cost of her spare pennies. She became an insatiable theatregoer, and soon passed from the operetta stage to the realistic drama.

And with that burden lifted, Rachel became ambitious. She thought of her future. She secured books; though she could read only Yiddish then, she naturally became interested in theatres, dramas, music, and soon, after having hummed songs many a time, she conceived the daring idea of presenting herself for admission to the theatre.

She had entered the romantic period, where the soul seeks a hero, or heroes, whom it proceeds to deify. Her hero was the rising Yiddish actor Russok. She had seen him as the leading juvenile, who was usually young, which was denoted by his appearing unshaven, and by his audacity. He always was good, sympathetic, adept in making love to women, impudent, but with a serious air about him.

She always attended the performances in which he had a sympathetic part. She felt certain that he, the great Russok, would help her realize her ambitions. She bought a number of plays, and learned the parts of the heroines by heart. She heard some of the songs so many times that she knew them by heart too. Then, one evening after the performance, she stationed herself at the stage entrance and waited with trembling.

After a number of portly chorus ladies had passed, Russok finally appeared. He looked about him casually, gave Rachel a keen glance and then paused to light a cigarette. That done, he looked at Rachel again and passed along. Rachel was too agitated to speak.

From thinking of her ambition, from dreaming about it, she had come to the point where she believed that without having her ambition satisfied she could not live. She discarded her timidity; she adopted the ways of the stage as far as she could, spent her money for little articles of adornment, although more necessary things had to be denied, and with a pertinacity worthy of a greater and better cause she set about catching the eye of the great Russok.

She wormed out of the doorkeeper at the stage entrance the address of Russok, and one morning she went up to 8th Street, where he lived.

Russok was a tall, angular young man, with a head of bushy black hair. When his housekeeper announced a young lady, he had at once covered his trousers and shirt with a heavy red dressing gown. He was now ready for public inspection.

Rachel was ushered in and took a seat near the door. Russok glanced at her casually, asking permission to smoke and then, spreading himself luxuriously on a couch, he inquired:

"What can I do for you?"

Rachel turned pale; the moment before she had blushed, but now that she had finally come to the end of her goal, her strength deserted her. She started to speak, but could only stammer and mumble. Russok arose and with a gallant gesture said:

"Have a glass of water, please."

She accepted the glass of water he handed her with a trembling hand and felt much relieved. Before she had gone vary far with her story Russok raised his head and inquired:

"You want to go upon the stage, is it not so?"

Rachel nodded her head.

"Then you will answer my questions," he said, "and we shall get along much better. You have never been on the stage before?"

"No, sir," she replied, sinking into her chair.

"You have never appeared in public?" he asked.

"Never," she said inaudibly.

"Then the only place you could go," he said, "would be in the chorus."

"Even that I would like," she answered timidly.

"But to go into the chorus you must belong to the union," he said.

"I can do that, can't I?" she inquired.

"That is the question," he said. "Our chorus is composed of heavyweight men and women whose only recommendation is that they belong to a union, and can force the manager to take them. To admit a new member is something unheard of. You can't displace one, and you can't add one."

"That is terrible," said Rachel, her heart sinking.

"But if you don't mind," said Russok, rising and coming closer to her, accidentally brushing her hair, "you come around and see me in a week, and it may be, with my influence, I shall be able to do something."

When he came close to her, Rachel felt her heart beating under her corset with great rapidity. She looked up to him with trembling, and when he told her to go, she could not trust herself to look straight at him. It was with downcast eyes she left him. He shut the door behind her, laughed, and lit another cigarette.

The week passed very slowly and Rachel feverishly awaited a summons from Russok. At last it came. She was asked to come over to see him the next morning at his room. She dressed herself with great care. That she was pretty, neatly dressed, chic, and very attractive, she knew when she glanced at herself in the mirror. It was the same room, the same Russok, and the same smile.

He was now more friendly. He asked her to remove her cloak. He helped her remove it, and looked at her with evident admiration. Rachel was not accustomed to such looks; they made her feel ill at ease; yet they pleased her.

"We are going to put on an operetta; it will require a number of extra chorus people," he said. "I have persuaded the manager to give you a trial. What do you think of that?"

Rachel could not speak; the news was overpowering. Her lips moved, but her tears had to speak her gratitude and joy.

He came close to her and advised her to take it easy; what he had done wasn't so much, but she had attracted him from the first, and he wanted to do something for her.

While speaking he sat down close to her and held her hand; she could feel his warm breath on her shoulder—and now she was afraid to speak.

Then he bent down closer and kissed her. At once she started up, her large black eyes, filled with tears of joy, flashing brilliantly. She wanted to speak angry words, but she could not.

His manner changed at once. He had gone far enough. The matter could wait. So, with reassuring words but without apology, he now quietly began advising her whom to see, how to go about the matter, and expressing the hope that he would see her again more often.

She was too much taken up with rehearsals and with the study of songs and with her general curiosity about everything concerning the stage to think very much of Russok during the following few weeks. At last she was going to be given a chance. Her disappointments were many. She was harried and hurried and subjected to the rough handling of men, but she did not complain. She was learning. She learned many things, some of them not pleasant; but through it all she felt that Russok was there to protect her. He stood some distance away, and his look seemed to give her that assurance.

As soon as she felt secure in her position she left her home and took up with one of the older girls in the company, who had learned much, but never anything of any value to her business as a chorus girl.

Rachel appeared on the stage, and her fresh voice and neat appearance made an impression, although she was in the chorus; for any girl among the ponderous group of coryphees in the company would be distinguished if she were half as pretty as Rachel Etienne, who was then in the first flush of an exuberant youth, and whom work on the stage had made an enthusiast.

Russok stood aloof, but soon, by little hints and a number of serious remarks, made Rachel feel that his interest in her continued. Once he took her to a café after the performance, and hinted that it was due to him that she remained where she was. He advised her to study, and told her that with the same influences she might become a legitimate actress.

He invited her, one evening when both were off duty, to one of the American theatres. After the performance and some coffee, he walked down the street with her in the direction of her home. Suddenly he stopped and took her hand.

"This can go on no longer," he said in a tragic voice.

"What is it?" she asked, alarmed.

"You need not ask me," he said. "You know. Ever since

I met you your image has been with me, following me around, and I cannot rid myself of it. I love you, and you should know it."

"You love me!" she cried. She thought she knew. She waited.

"I love you, and only you," he said, in a low voice. "When you first came to see me I felt that you were the destined one. I cannot rest without you. I am constantly thinking of you."

She took his arm, and for a while, as they walked, she did not speak. Then she looked up into his face and said:

"I love you."

He stopped and, indifferent to the passers-by, kissed her passionately. They then resumed their walk, and thereafter spoke as if nothing unusual had happened, although Rachel felt a curious thumping about her heart.

"Well, what shall we do?" he asked.

"What do you think?" she said.

"There is one thing; we ought to get married," he said.

"Yes, we ought to get married," she said.

"There is one thing I must tell you; you must know it, my dear," he said, somewhat confused.

"Tell me," she said.

"It is awkward to say it," he said. "But you must know. When I came over to this country, five years ago, I was young, I was ignorant, but—I had already been married."

"I don't care what you have been," she said softly.

"I mean—you don't understand—I mean I am married now," he said.

"You have a wife?" she asked, her voice rising, suddenly removing her arm.

"You must listen to me," he said hurriedly. "It was an arranged match. My mother would have it. I haven't seen

or heard from her for five years. I don't want to hear of her.
I have written to her, offering a divorce. She has not answered. Wife or no wife, I love you."

Rachel walked along by his side, silent. He walked along,
moodily, now and then glancing at her. She loved him.
She knew of the premature matches contracted in Russia
between children. She knew that it seldom, at the time,
meant anything. He would marry her if he could.

"Let us get married in court," she finally said.

"If I did and my wife came here and showed her marriage certificate I would be a bigamist." he said.

"Then what shall we do?" she asked.

"I love you; you love me," he replied, speaking as if the
words choked him. "Let us live together and when I can
get my wife to take a divorce from me, we shall be married."

Rachel loved and trusted him, and when he insisted that
nothing of a public nature attend their nuptials, she agreed,
and though they lived as man and wife, the little world in
which they moved about knew nothing of it, or, at most, only
suspected, and held its tongue.

For a time Rachel was happy. She made rapid progress.
Then, at the height of her career, there came a disturbing
force of nature—pregnancy. When she spoke of it to Russok
he was startled, but managed to pretend to be pleased. She
saw he was troubled, and soon noticed with terror that he
no longer showed the same interest in her and in the little
troubles that soon came, until in short order his indifference became neglect, and when she was compelled to leave
the stage for a while he seemed to be as indifferent as though
they had been no more than friends.

During her heaviest period she heard nothing from him.
The few dollars she had saved she spent to prepare for her

child. He did not contribute any more. Then she became
indifferent to him. The child was born without a father to
welcome it. Rachel conceived a great hatred for the man.
Her love became hateful to her, and she lost it. She could
not bear to think that such a cruel man should have a share
in her child. She did not want to have him claim a share.
She wanted the boy all to herself.

When she recovered she returned to the stage. She was
welcomed by the manager and the company, and they asked
no questions. Nor did Russok ask any questions. His public
demeanor toward her had always been correct. He always
wore his public demeanor now.

Once Russok met her in the long underground passage
that led onto the stage, alone, and he could not avoid her.
She stepped aside to let him pass. He stopped and said:

"You are looking pretty again, do you know, Rachel?"

She looked at him with disdain, but he continued:

"I wouldn't mind," he said, "coming up to see you once
in a while if you invited me."

She came closer to him and raised her hand. He received
a resounding slap on one cheek, and as he raised his hand
to cover it he received another on the other cheek. When
he recovered his composure, Rachel was not to be seen.

At the end of the season Rachel left the company and
went to London with Dikman. In London Rachel Etienne
did not make a great success, but winning the favor of one
of those pursuers of oddities who infest all capitals, she was
sent at his expense to Paris to study the art of acting. There,
thanks to other persons interested in her, she learned the
technical elements of the art, which she had lacked, and
when she made her debut as a serious actress she im-

mediately won a place for herself in the center of dramatic
art, Paris.

She had her further disillusionments, but she also enjoyed
life and acquired wisdom. She cultivated a cynical manner,
combined with good nature, which was fetching to the
highest degree. Her son was already half-grown when she
left Paris for her first engagement in New York. She had
already captivated London, Berlin, Vienna, and St. Petersburg. Now, urged on by friends, she wanted to conquer the
New World. And conquer it she did.

One evening she expressed a desire to see a play performed
in one of the foreign theatres of New York.

The German theatre was suggested.

"Ah! those Germans. I cannot bear to see them in this
beautiful city also," she laughed.

The performance of an Italian company was proposed.

"I have seen too many of them," she said.

A performance by a Jewish company was suggested, given
in a theatre built by Jews, owned by Jews, and in a play
written by a Jew.

"That is good, my friend," she said. "I also am a Jewess.
I shall see my compatriots act."

A box was reserved for her, and with a company of friends,
including myself, she saw the performance of one of Manewitz's dramas.

In the company, of which Ritter was the star, was Russok.
He played the part of an old man. I noticed that Madame
Rachel was strangely interested in him, and when, between
the acts, I asked an usher I knew what Russok's standing
was, the young man said:

"He is out of date. He can play only old men now. Once
he was a rising actor. But he became fat; his voice cracks,

and he doesn't understand modern methods. He still clings to the Lecker method, but Lecker, although he lives, is as good as dead, so what's the use? A back number, take my word for it!"

I said nothing to Madame Rachel. But after the performance she expressed a desire to visit Graff, in whom she saw a talent she admired. She was received in Ritter's dressing-room. He arose when she came in, made a low bow, and uttered words of homage. Madame Rachel said a few words of praise, suggested that his art should depend less upon the mood of the moment and more upon study, and then asked to see the man who had played the father. Ritter, somewhat put out, ordered Russok to be called for. Russok's face had lost its beauty, its form and grace, and there was a looseness about his mouth which was repellent.

Madame Rachel raised her lorgnette to her eyes and stared at him. He stood there in astonishment, and then, as he recognized her, was about to speak when Madame Rachel held up her hand.

"Do not speak!" she said. "I command you. You will understand me. It is to you I speak, and I wish my friends to hear what I say."

He bowed, and she said to the amazed actor:

"I owe you much. I thank God that my son does not know you. It is better he should meet men who have only the average amount of wickedness. An actor speaks through the parts he plays. You probably have not been able to play anything that demands nobility, self-sacrifice, and honor. You play what you are—a poltroon."

No one spoke as we left, It was some time before we regained our composure and Madame Rachel was herself again. While she was in New York she never went to another Jewish theatre.

XI

Inspiration—Alcoholic

SOLATEV SAT IN A DINGY COFFEE-HOUSE ON SECOND AVENUE with his head resting on his palms. He cursed in a medley of back alley phrases taken from a variety of languages and literatures. He cursed his days and he cursed his nights, he cursed his father and his mother, the managers and the actors—and his own perverse luck. For Solatev was strapped and had not had a drink for about eight hours. That accounted for his depression.

He was surrounded by a group of excited, keen-eyed gamblers, who shuffled cards, puffed at long cigars, drank beer in quick gulps, and kept their eyes on the man who was dealer at the moment. The waiter did not know Solatev; replenished his glass—with tea—eyed him suspiciously and threw questioning glances at the players.

On the street, troops of children danced in circles; girls in their best attire promenaded; stout mothers took the air with their offspring; and a hand-organ filled the air with

155

German music. It was sultry, but not unpleasant—except to Solatev, who, wrestling with his life's problem, found it a perspiration-inducing effort.

His pockets were frayed and empty. He saw before him a prospect of doing without liquor for another day, not to speak of doing without his hall bedroom and the food required to stabilize the tea he could afford to consume. It was a dismal outlook.

Solatev wrote plays so easily that he often wondered why playwriting was called an art. He wrote comedies, melodramas, tragedies, operettas; he had no preferences or specialties. And his plays were distinguished for one quality. You could not tell from whom they had been stolen. Other plagiarists were not so adept; the stolen goods betrayed their origin. Solatov gave his plots a manner which was all his own. His plays came through the sieve of his own mind, touched by a wild imagination and in intuitive knack for effects; he knew how to touch the heart—the soft heart, at any rate.

But his were not regarded as good plays. In this respect, also, there was no distinction, for the Yiddish theatre had many bad playwrights. There was always a good human story in what Solatev wrote, but the finished product lacked what actors called strength; the good points bulged out brutally; but the general level was low. "He lacks soul," said the now sedate Mme. Lessin. "His words haven't got density," said Burlak. "There's no salt and pepper in them," said Ritter, haughtily.

And that was why Solatev was merely an emergency playwright. If a new production proved a failure and there was nothing else on hand, Solatev was a last refuge of distracted managers. At the end of the season, when novelties could not be wasted in hazardous sacrifice, Solatev was often called upon to fill the gap.

You may be sure that Solatev never rolled in the lap of luxury. His protest was expressed in libations to Bacchus. In consuming liquor Solatev was an adept. It was not easy for him to become drunk; but when he was filled to the brim, all the pepper and salt, all the density of speech, all the vigor, all the soul which he was said to lack came to him and his pudgy face became as red as a beet, and his eyes sparkled, and his friends then said:

"It's too bad he doesn't write a play when he's dead drunk! That might be a play!"

As he listened vaguely to the tumult of the gamesters, he saw the stout form of Levin, the prompter, passing, and at once shouted his name and beckoned to him. Levin turned, and his face betrayed a smile. He made his way into the basement and after shaking hands with him formally, sat down at the table with Solatev.

"What are you doing in this joint?" he asked.

"As you see," replied Solatev, gruffly. "I am cursing the day I was born. I have also cursed Ritter, and Burlak, the Yiddish theatre, Second Avenue, and now I don't know whom next to curse."

"Give him a highball," Levin ordered the waiter.

"If I could only be a house writer in a music-hall," said Solatev, drinking. "But I have no luck!"

"Haven't you got anything on hand?" asked Levin.

"When haven't I anything on hand?" said Solatev. "In my trunk I have ideas for a hundred plays, but the trouble is more serious."

"Aren't the plays good?" asked Levin.

"I am the victim of a damned conspiracy," said Solatev. "They don't want my original plays. All they want is imitations. Ritter wants my plays to be like Manewitz's. Burlak wants them to be like Krolik's. I have longings to be original, to be different. Which means that they won't have anything

of mine as long as I am myself. Which means that I'll have
to quit being myself in order to be a playwright. I am bound
in a magic circle."

"The trouble with you is that you haven't got guts
enough," said Levin. "Your plays are good, but not good
enough. Your scenes are strong, but not strong enough. You
must put ginger in your stuff."

"Ritter says salt and pepper," said Solatev moodily.

"Whatever you call it," said Levin, "you must put it into
your stuff or you're as good as dead; or go into the music-
hall business, where you'll have to write forty new plays a
season for thirty dollars a week."

"Your warning don't do me any good," said Solatev.
"What I need now is a stake."

He assumed the manner of a man about to negotiate a
loan. Levin appreciated the maneuver. "How much?" he
asked, frowning.

"Make it five," replied Solatev. "You can afford to let me
take that trifle. You're single; you've a place all season; and
aren't you a good friend of mine?"

"I'll let you have five on one condition," said Levin.

"What is it?" Solatev queried.

"That you make up your mind once more to write a
play in the style of Manewitz and Lecker, only to show
them that you can beat them at their own game. But let it
be original, you hear?"

"Make it ten, and I'll try," was Solatev's answer.

They left the coffee-house together, Levin going in the
direction of 14th Street. As Solatev walked down Second
Avenue, he gave thought to Levin's suggestion, and wondered what he could do to retrieve his fortunes. He held
the ten-dollar bill in his fist. Suddenly he seemed to have
made a discovery. He walked rapidly and entered Forsyth

Street, going in the direction of Marcus's cafe. When he entered that rendezvous he quickly espied in the corner the man he was seeking. It was Lonkes, Ritter's brother-in-law.

"How are you, Solatev?" inquired Lonkes, pushing back his slouch hat from his forehead.

"I want to speak to you particularly," said Solatev.

Lonkes was a beau. His style was the envy of all players with any pretension to social distinction—his spats, hats, vests, ties, and colored handkerchiefs. He had all the manners of a woman in his taste in clothes. But he was also a patron of art. Lacking creative ability, he overcame his frustrations by being generous to those who had talent.

"I am going to do something, and I need your help," said Solatev to Lonkes when they arrived at City Hall, where they sat down on a bench.

"What are you going to do?" inquired, Lonkes, feeling for his wallet.

"I am going," said Solatev soberly, "to get drunk."

"But that's nothing unusual," remarked Lonkes, laughing. "Whenever you are in doubt, you get drunk."

"I'm never drunk enough," said Solatev. "I always get just about ten feet away from intoxication, and then, because I have no more money, I can go no further. I never get to the end of the road. I want you to do me a favor."

"What is the favor?" asked Lonkes, amused.

"Come and take care of me; and get me what I need," said Solatov.

"Get me as many plays and novels as you can. I'll provide the liquor," he said.

"What do you mean?"

"I'm going to write a play with pepper and salt and ginger in it," said Solatev. "But I must be stiff drunk, and have my head filled with ideas for plays. If they want imitations

from me, I can give them an imitation that will beat anything the Yiddish theatre ever had."

"I'll do anything for art," said Lonkes.

He hired a room for Solatev, had a few bottles of whiskey
sent up to it, provided him with a number of pads, brought
in a few dozen plays and novels, and shut the door on him.
He directed a waiter to bring Solatev anything he asked for,
but not to let him out.

Solatev said good-bye to Levin a few nights later and
went to his den. He drank himself into a fine state of exhilaration and began to read, with relish and discernment. He
swallowed Lessing and Grillparzer, Pinero and George Ob-
net, until he felt his gorge rising at the literary mess he had
absorbed. Then he went to sleep. In the morning he had a
light breakfast and continued his quest. He found his body
tingling all over. His mind seemed so alert, so filled with
fancy, that he determined, should fortune turn favorably
to him, that he would ever after devote one day in ten to
Bacchus, undeterred by menial labor. He seemed to com-
prehend the dramatists he read with marvelous intuition. As
he drank he spread the wings of his fancy, he ruminated
over the visions created by the playwrights he was reading,
and on the second day of his debauch he took up his pen
and began to write.

He seemed to see the mechanism of the stage with an un-
canny insight. He felt the pulse of the audience in every
line he wrote. He remembered what Ritter and Burlak
wanted of him, and he wove the plot into a form which
gave each act its melodrama, its comedy, its pathos, its ap-
peal to the intellect. When he was at a loss for invention
his mind, brilliantly alive, at once presented to him inci-
dents from the novels and plays he had just read, and he
found himself putting together a play that had all the good

qualities of all the plays he had read, plus vigor, plus salt and pepper and soul.

He reveled in the world of fiction. He saw how wretched had been his existence until he had treated his body to this alcoholic bath. He saw before him a world of imagination, and he twisted the novels he read and the plays he perused to suit his own wild fancy. He imagined to himself the characters of the classic world, and refashioned the speeches they had made which were embedded in the printed works of Shakespeare, Lessing, and Schiller. He lashed himself into a fury of imaginative revelry, and in the evening of the third day fell exhausted and slept for twelve hours. When he awoke, his mind was still in a quiver of excitement, and he proceeded with the third act.

In five days he had completed the play. Lonkes, who hovered about his door every evening, put his ear to the keyhole on that day, and hearing a heavy, stertorous breathing, opened the door and entered. He saw Solatev fast asleep, with a peaceful smile on his lips, and a few dozen empty bottles scattered about the room. On the table, carefully arranged, was a manuscript, on the top of which was written, "Guilty, a Drama in Four Acts."

It took twenty-four hours for Solatev to come to himself. Without reading the play he had written, he took the manuscript to Lonkes and said:

"Advance me one hundred dollars, sell this play, and take it out of what you get for it."

"Where are you going?" asked Lonkes.

"I am going to the country," replied Solatev.

"How do I know the play is any good?" asked Lonkes.

"You can rely upon it—I was never so drunk in all my life," replied Solatev.

Lonkes gave him sixty dollars and Solatev went to the Catskill Mountains to spend the summer.

Lonkes looked for a purchaser of the drama. He gave Ritter first choice, but he would not have it.

"I've read the play," said Ritter, "but there is something suspicious about it."

"How's that?"

"Well, it reminds me of other plays, but I can't tell which," said Ritter.

"You needn't take it then," said Lonkes, and left in a huff.

He went over to see Burlak, who knew nothing of dramatic literature, had never read the classic masterpieces and knew nothing of Ibsen, Dumas, Pinero, and who, when he had read Solatev's drunken production, smacked his lips.

"I always said that this drunkard would write a masterpiece some day," he said to Lonkes. "The play has words that you can bite into, and it rings like true melodrama, and it has room for comedy, and——What does he want for it?"

"You like it, eh? Then we'll come to terms," said Lonkes. "Solatev is now in the dump; you can name your own figure for it."

Solatev returned to New York, emaciated and haggard, for in the country, with all his money going for board and lodgings, he seldom approached a state of intoxication that was even slightly satisfying. He had meandered about the country place, "kibitzed" about the gaming tables (being too poor to play), and returned to New York with a long-unsatisfied thirst that was just aching to be nourished. He at once made a levy on Lonkes, who readily advanced money on the strength of the contract with Burlak.

"Guilty" was to be the first offering of the season. Burlak's company spoke of it with reverence. They were given fine opportunities to display their talents. The text was full of strong, vibrant words. The situations were enthralling. Burlak expected to have "Guilty" run for the season and engaged Shmulewitz to write special music for it, to provide a few songs to be interpolated if necessary. He had his orchestra compose decorative melodies to be used at discretion. He had an entirely new setting for one of the acts. His costumer was plagued to provide the very best costumes. But Solatev was not in evidence at any of the rehearsals. He was too drunk to be interested. He had abandoned the child of his brain at Burlak's doorstep.

A few days after the first performance, the dramatic critic of the "Daily Sheker" reviewed the play. He praised it, but ended his account with this significant paragraph:

"The fact that it is a good play raises a doubt as to its authorship. The program gives the name of Solatev. A correction is suggested. Solatev's name should be erased, and in its place the following should be inserted: Pinero for the first act and Scribe for the comedy in it; Dumas for the second act, with Fulda for the sentiment; the American Clyde Fitch for the comedy, and Sudermann for the climax, with William Gillette for the technique of the climax, which appears in "Held by the Enemy"; the Socialist Mirabeau for the third act with credit to Goldfaden for the comedy, Manewitz for the pathos, and again Clyde Fitch for the climax. The last act, in justice, should be attributed to all the writers above mentioned, who are strangely jumbled together."

When Burlak read the "Sheker" that day he became virtuously indignant. He sent for Lonkes, who came over to his theatre post-haste.

"I am surprised at you," said Burlak "—that a man of your literary judgment should have perpetrated a fraud on

a manager, palming off a plagiarism as an original work. I
have had nothing to do with that sot Solatev, but with you.
Is it fair to hold me up to ridicule in the Yiddish press?"

"My dear Burlak," replied Lonkes, stretching himself
languidly in a chair, "what you purchased you had a chance
to read. 'Let the buyer beware' is the legal maxim."

"But between you and me, why should I pay for an
adapted play the same as for an original?" said Burlak. "Let
us come to some agreement. I don't want to keep on paying
that fellow Solatev royalties this season. I don't want to be
bothered with him. I'll settle with him for a lump sum and
be done with it."

"I'll have to consult with Solatev," said Lonkes. "What
is your price?"

"Five hundred dollars," said Burlak cautiously.

"Anything else?" asked Lonkes.

"I shall have to take his name off the billboards," remarked Burlak, "if they keep on calling the play a plagiarism."

Lonkes went out in search of the errant Solatev. He could
not be found in any of the cafés, nor was he in his room.
Lonkes was at a loss where to go when Levin hove in sight.
Lonkes asked him whether he knew where Solatev could be
found.

"He is on a spree," said Levin with a smile.

"But where can I find him?" asked Lonkes.

Levin mentioned the name of a resort on 15th Street. He
found Solatev tipsy, supported by a brace of girls, who
seemed to have him in their clutches. There were glasses on
the table. (Women were another weakness of Solatev that
should be mentioned; but not at this time.)

"I want to talk business with you, Solatev," said Lonkes.
"Let's get out of here."

"I'm ready to talk business any time," Solatev said with a leer. "Have you got any money for me? This is my banker," he said to the girls.

"Are you willing to sell your play for three hundred dollars?" asked Lonkes, anxious to finish a disagreeable task.

"Three hundred dollars?" echoed Solatev.

"Take the cash and let the credit go," said the sober girl.

"Right you are," said Solatev, rising.

He signed the contract and Lonkes left him in the den.

He ran through the three hundred dollars in a few weeks and returned, conscience-stricken and gloomy, to his former haunt. The first poster he saw was an announcement of the play "Guilty." He looked intently for the name of the author. He saw "Professor Jacoby from London" given as the "renowned author." "Professor Jacoby" was the vicarious author of all the shameless adaptations and plagiarisms of the Yiddish theatre. Solatev rushed to see Lonkes.

"You're a fool, Solatev," said Lonkes, after listening to his imprecations. "Let Professor Jacoby be the author of that bastard play. Why should you give your name to such rot?"

Solatev was too befuddled to fight any more. His mind was settled. He would cease having aspirations. He would return to the hack work of writing plays and sell them wherever there was a market. When he received an order to write a four-act melodrama for a music-hall, he drank himself into another fit of intoxication. But no inspiration ever came to guide his pen again. He wrote his mongrel plays for a number of years. They were in a class by themselves. Then he disappeared, and it was said that he had been found asleep in a hallway in a Bowery resort. From that sleep he could not be aroused. He had passed out, never to revive again.

XII

Dahlman's Play

IT IS A DOMAIN INVENTED BY EXILES WHO DREAM OF THE LAND of their hearts' desire; they call it Bohemia.

In the particular Bohemia of our fancy, Schiffman and I were seated, sipping tea, which is a favorite beverage. Schiffman is a specialist in the Yiddish drama. He plays with the masks of the Yiddish theatre.

The subject of our conversation was, of course, Bohemian news—the latest play, the art exhibit, the newest poet and the daringest book; and the deep significance of Manewitz's "Gott, Mensch und Teufel," the like of which has not been seen since Goethe's "Faust," which it imitates. As we sipped our third glass Schiffman raised his head and hailed a young man who had just entered. He was a slim, spare young fellow with jet-black hair, a long face, and a prominent nose. His deep-set eyes were shadowed by glasses. He wore a wrinkled overcoat and a turned-down collar with a flowing black necktie. His shoulders twitched, as if he meant to hold himself erect but could not.

He returned Schiffman's salute and, after casting a glance over the room and evidently not finding what he was looking for, he seated himself at our table without invitation or introduction. It is rudeness to take offense at such conduct (in Bohemia). Ordering a glass of tea and running his hand through his hair, he broke into our conversation with:

"Say! I've got one of the finest ideas you ever heard of! It's been buzzing in my head for ever so long. Even now, while it is not so clear as it will be later, it stands out as a fine idea. You've got to hear it!"

Experienced as a Bohemian gentleman, Schiffman expressed no astonishment at this outburst, but said indifferently:

"If you've got anything on your mind, Dahlman, fire away."

Dahlman's eyes gleamed with excitement. His fingers pinched and twisted the cigarette he was smoking. He seemed to swell with enthusiasm. He pressed both elbows on the table, hunched his shoulders, cleared his throat, and began.

"It sticks in my mind for the last few days as a one-act play. If I had told it to somebody, it might have developed into something else; it might have reshaped itself, it might have become a three-act play; but there it is, wedged in my mind, focussed for good, it seems, as a one-act play. I have tried all forms: I have moulded it into a short story, a poem, an essay, an allegory—you don't know how much thought I have given to it—but it won't budge. A one-act play it must be. . . .

"I want you to see a medium-sized stage, set to picture one of your old-fashioned garrets. You've read of them in French romances—places where artists have their ambitions knocked out of them, where wretchedness is endured in the name of some artistic ideal—music, painting, poetry, drama. The walls of the garret are bare, except for a few panels, a few unfinished pictures, old clothes, old easels, piled up in one corner. You will also see a couch, a table with a wax taper on it, a bookcase, etc. The ceiling comes down near the floor in the rear, and you see a skylight, through it the spires of a church, or the roofs of buildings, or the city in silhouette. The setting is all drab.

"When the curtain rises, it is night. A young man enters, drags himself wearily across the room and stumbles into a chair. Outdoors, it is raining, one of those dismal, chilly rains. You will hear the swish of the rain on the skylight.

"He is an art student, but why an art student only the God who made him knows. Before he came to Paris he had a longing to devote himself to art. Art is evasion of life. His eyes could not become used to reality. This longing had grown in his soul until the desire to see 'Carcassonne' had overpowered him, and he set out for the center of art and squalor. He suffers poverty, but struggles on; he suffers isolation, but struggles on. And he is no nearer his goal now than when he first came—he does know clearly what his goal may be. His face invites compassion.

"That's the young fellow. When he moves from the chair and throws himself upon the couch the stage is flooded with darkness. You will ask—I can see that—how can it be flooded with darkness? That's an ingenious idea of my own. I'll not front the calcium light with a red or blue screen. I shall have it fronted with a thick black screen, which will naturally exclude all other rays of light and cast the stage into pitch darkness. It will be thick with darkness.

"And when the stage is steeped in darkness, the music of the overture will merge into the music of the play. It will

be music in which, at first, the ideas will be scattered, dis-
cordant, harsh, swelling and retreating—dark, somber music.
You will feel as if the stage is the scene of strange develop-
ments, as if a complete, mysterious, meaningful idea is about
to be born; as if some dreadful, inexplicable clairvoyance is
to be perpetrated. The music will grow to a giant wave.
It will move the audience to wonder. It will be awed by the
conflicting waves of sound until—slowly with deliberation,
persuasively with magnificence, out of the chaos of sound,
out of the birth-pangs of the theme—harmony will emerge;
as if the discords, the scattered ideas, the struggling disunion,
were becoming reconciled, coalescing, swaying together, fus-
ing into one clear, vivid, soul-stirring, melancholy, dreadful
idea—which will rise majestically, sway in the air and almost
speak itself to the audience.

"And just as the idea is most clear, all its elements reconciled, when there is no mistaking its meaning, when it seems
to glow with vivid life, when it sways there steadily, you
will see, looking toward the couch, in the center of the
stage, a Face!

"If I could only describe it to you as I have seen it! It is
soft and mellow, but without emotion; cool, placid, suave,
steel-white—a face of peace which reflects quiet, deep-seated
maternal love; and yet it is masculine in its contour. It is
human, yet unhuman in its supernal beauty. It is a face
that expresses unutterable pity, and yet it is stern; just a
quiver of sternness, a ripple, passes over it now and then.

"All I have said until now is introductory. I have given
you the setting. Can you see it?

"The Face becomes clearer, more beautiful, and slowly
moves toward the boy. You can see no form (there is no
form), but you feel it. You see no hands (there are no
hands), but you feel them—cool, soothing. You know that

a hand has moved over the boy's face, and that he starts
from his sleep, though you see nothing until the light falls on
him. He gazes at the figure intently, then calmly, as if seeking to question it. But the figure speaks first. These are
the first words spoken in the play. It says:

" 'Do not shrink from me. I know you are weary of beating against the rocks. You have tried it these many months,
and you are where you may understand it; where the visions
of beauty you create may come true. Life and art are separated here, and life and its art are beyond you. Come where
you may find rest.'

"The boy replies:

" 'I have so much to do. I'm still looking for life, for life
that's beautiful, life that's worth while, life that doesn't
kill. It must be found somewhere. I'll find it yet!'

"The figure continues:

" 'You seek life here, where you will never find it. Life is
not for you. Over yonder, you shall find what you seek—
yonder, where all is peace, where dreams are the coin of the
realm, where vision rules. It is the way of life, though it
goes by another name. Follow me, and you may join the
throngs who have gone before, the great artists, the poets,
the creators of music, the great martyrs of the world. Come
with me!'

"The boy mutters:

" 'Not until I have met the enemy, face to face. I don't
know what obstructs my way. I don't know what life is. Let
me see it first! Let me fail; but let me see it for myself.'

"Then the figure says:

" 'Look behind you and see!'

"And then, in the center of the stage (for the two are
near the left, the left as you see it) you will see another
figure, but different—large, coarse, with muscles bulging out,

blood on its brow, sternly masculine, with scars, strong (offensively so), with a hard look on its face, a bludgeon in one hand—a monstrous, threatening, awful figure, panting, its chest moving heavily. It seems to have had a bath in red blood, which drips from its face, its arms, its body; and it stands in a pool of blood—all red! This mute presence will revolt the audience. There will be something overwhelming in its appearance, nauseating, everybody in the audience will find a partial reflection of himself in this monster, which will create great uneasiness, apprehension, which increases as the figure speaks.

" 'Do you see it?'

"The boy shudders, and mutters, 'Yes, yes' and then, fearfully, inquires of the new visitor:

" 'I have seen him before, but who he is I do not know. Oh, tell me why there is blood on your brow and a bludgeon in your hand? Why are you so scarred and stern? Are you life?"

"The second figure says, brazenly:

" 'I am not as many picture me, but I am none the less true. I am for the strenuous, who can bear both defeat and victory. I am for the callous, who make terms with me. I am the master of conflict; that is why you see scars on my face. I am the master of pain; that is why you see me defiant. I am the master of force; that is why you see this bludgeon in my hand. I am for the strong! I hate the puny, the nerveless, the sensitive; my skin is thick, you see? You atom, I know you! You are not destined to follow me. You halt, you hesitate, you cannot bear to look the sun in the face, you shun the struggle, you sicken at the smell of blood. I love it! Who would know me must abandon fear. You think to live and to evade me by building for yourself a world of dreams, the world of unreality. I shall shatter that world, I

shall reduce it to dust—for I hate and fight it. Your world
is the invention of my enemy—Death! I am for the active,
the strenuous, the unafraid!'

"Do you catch the idea? I want that to grip you. I want
you to look at that monster and be afraid. The details are of
no consequence: I can polish them up later.

"When the monster has spoken the boy rises, shrieks, and
rushes into the arms of the friendly visitor, who has been
standing by placidly, and exclaims:

" 'His look freezes me!'

"And he breaks into hysterics, laughs and sobs:

" 'I am no warrior: I can't stand the sight and smell of
blood. Take me to your world—take me with you!'

"The first figure bends down, soothingly, mournfully,
and with a glance of reproach toward the other figure, who
vanishes into the darkness, it says:

" 'That is why I came. And you will not regret it. But
be quiet. You must sleep. You must think of pleasant things,
of the world as you would have it, of your dream-world.
And it shall come true. All things are true when you believe in them.'

"It places him on the couch and covers him, maternally,
until you see that the boy has fallen asleep in its arms.

"Then—a thunderous crash! The stage is in complete
darkness again!

"And the same musical idea you heard before, which
preceded the coming of the first figure, returns, full, as if it
had been in retirement and now reappears pregnant to the
verge of bursting. It swells in volume, sways a while,
as if its mission had been accomplished and it knew not
whither to turn. Then with a great upheaval, it breaks into
millions of fragments—discords—harsh, fearful, wild out-
bursts of sound. The discords are at war with one another,

regretting their temporary union. They break, scatter, lose force, subside. They creep out of the crevices of the garret, through the skylight, out into the open, over the housetops; they fade away into the distance, far away, as if taking something with them. They will die away into an inaudible whisper. Their departure will relieve the audience, who will feel that they have passed through a great, exhausting struggle. Their own thoughts will be reflected in it. The death of the music will mean the cessation of all disturbing ideas. The darkness will then lift. Through the skylight (only the skylight) a bright light will appear. The sun is rising. Its rays will fall upon the boy's face. He is fast asleep. He does not move. In all probability he is dead. You can have it either way.

"Isn't that a finely chiseled idea?"

"The people won't like it," said Schiffman.

"I never can understand when I am referred to popular opinion! What do you think of it?"

"I like it," said Schiffman, rather coldly.

"Glad you do, at any rate. But don't forget it is my idea," said Dahlman, and with an abrupt wave of the hand to the waiter, whom he had not paid for the tea, adjusted his overcoat with the same curious twitch of the shoulders, ran his hand through his hair, and rushed out.

"Who's that fellow?" I inquired, amazed. "Dahlman? I've never heard that name before. Has he written anything?"

"Not a line," said Schiffman.

"What?"

"He does not write. If he does, he writes with invisible ink and you must follow the movements of his pen to see his work. He gives away his ideas as soon as they inspire him. He glows with an idea, good or bad, and tells it to a friend, and that's the death of it for him. He is filled with the ashes of defunct compositions; he has been jammed with the most curious fantasies, but he cannot hold them. He is jammed with miscarriages. He kills them by giving them air. He always thinks he will turn back and write them down, polish them up, but he never returns. He loses the magic word to bring back his own children. He has told us this allegory of life and death profusely, but with such sincerity in the telling that you are moved—you, a Bohemian! But he will never tell it again. Should you wish to use it, as you please, in play or poem; in music or dance; it's yours for the taking. He will never claim or recognize it. He is a Bohemian, at any rate, and there is no copyright law in Bohemia."

When I had reconsidered the matter later, after I had returned to the land of the Philistines, I confess I saw nothing impressive about the tale. It was Dahlman who had given vividness and distinction to his "drama." He had made me see a picture that could not be expressed in paint or words. There was nothing else to it.

XIII

Knockers at the Door

YACHSON IS NOW A RETIRED PLAYWRIGHT; HE LEFT THE THEA-
tre in a huff and refused to struggle for dramatic honors.
He writes no more. His muse is silent. But he may be tipped
any evening at Shullem's café on Division Street, where he
serves the patrons of that rendezvous of wit and idleness
with distinguished grace.

But he is a disappointed man. His wiry black mustache
has been trained downward. He smiles in a wan, impersonal
manner, and his comments on the status of the Yiddish
drama are loftily disparaging.

("My dear Yachson," you say to him as he places a glass of
steaming tea before you, "why deprecate that which, in the
estimation of the intelligent and in your own, has absolutely
no value? Speak well of the dead."

He shakes his head. "You see, I had hopes of reviving it,"
he says, "but when they kicked all my high hopes into the
gutter, when they slammed the door in my face and rejected

175

the best drama I ever wrote, I decided there was no use hoping any more. The Yiddish theatre is doomed to remain in the gutter where it has fallen, and whoever helps bury it will be doing a service to the East Side, to the Theatre and the world in general."

It is about two in the morning. His voice quivers with emotion, resentment, and wounded vanity, as he lays bare his heart. It is a case of genius neglected, spurned and despoiled.)

This is the story he told:

I have seen almost every play produced in the Yiddish theatres. I have read Ibsen, Sudermann, Bernard Shaw, Manewitz and Shakespeare. I know all the Yiddish actors and managers and dramatists. You'll excuse me, then, if I say that I may qualify as a student of the drama, if not more. I understand technique, life, literature, and, what is more important, I understand the managers, and the actors who hold the destinies of the Yiddish theatre in their palms, as it were. For years, over in Zeitlen's restaurant, I used to hear talking about the Yiddish drama men like Manewitz, who wrote "God, Man and Devil"; Grobyan, who wrote "The Black Paradise"; Kahn, editor of "The Forwards"; and Herr Ritter and Herr Burlak, both of them distinguished players. I read Fusher's theatrical magazine as long as he had the impudence and the money to publish it, and before that I used to read Gordin's ill-fated theatrical magazine, which I knew (I may say) by heart. So you see, I understand the Yiddish theatre.

What was more natural than that I should sit down and write a play? True, I am only a waiter, but what was Lecker before he became a writer of cheap melodrama? He was an usher, a hanger-on in Rumanian cafés, a gambler. What

was Grobyan before he wrote plays? He was a slovenly cigar-
maker. What was that anemic and cowardly Krolik but a
vender of newspapers in the Bronx?

So I too wrote a play. This is free America, anyway. It
was in five acts, and had fifteen characters in it. Before I
finished it I conferred with Kahn, who told me it would be
better to cut it down to seven characters; better for the pro-
ducer, he said. He also advised me to reduce the number
of scenes to five, one for each act, instead of fifteen, three
for each act; also better for the manager. Not having a
swelled head, and thinking of the manager's interest as well
as my own, I did what Kahn advised me. I was also thinking
that if I did what he told me, I could count on "The Forwards" for a good review.

The labor I put into that play is beyond words to describe.
I actually sweated all through it. I must have used up
hundreds of pounds of good wrapping paper. I didn't sleep
nights. I was so absent-minded that I almost lost my job.
My wife cursed me roundly every morning for taking up a
business I didn't understand, and because of it she turned
her attention to admirers, outings, and God knows what.
But I couldn't think of anything but that play for three
months. In short, the drama was written under conditions
that would have discouraged any man of talent.

Need I tell you what kind of play came out? Of course,
it was a problem play; but I took good care to put in scenes
for the comedian Badchen, so that he could improvise his
well-known jests. And there were situations that offered
room for Burlak's heroics, and emotional scenes for Madame
Lessin to wriggle through in her oriental manner. There
were parts for every member of a stock company—places
where they could use good, substantial words, words they
could put their teeth into; conflicts, denunciations, appeals

to the gallery—every essential for a successful play was there. It was called "The Sins of the Mothers."

Then I began to peddle my play. Every actor and manager knew I had written a play—I was diplomatic enough to tell them all—but not one took the initiative and made me an offer or asked me to read it for his benefit. Well, they didn't come to me; so I went to them.

The disappointments, the humiliations, the ignominy of it! To submit a problem play to such ignoramuses! In one of the scenes I had the villain leave the stage, and the directions were, "Exit villain, and as he closes the door behind him he says to himself, 'Now I have the fool on the hip.' " They asked me "What use is it for him to say that to himself, off stage?" Do you appreciate to what depths of ignorance they have fallen in the production of Yiddish plays?

I had a beautiful scene for Badchen, the comedian, and of course I left the dialogue blank. The stage directions were, "Here Badchen cracks some of his side-splitting jokes." One manager asked me, "What jokes?" More in sorrow than in anger I said, "Do you suppose I'm going to compete with the great comedian Badchen in the making of jokes?"

I had the heroine poison herself in the last act. She had no alternative. But, instead of taking the poison on the stage, and telling her husband what she had done, and thus making a mess of things, I had her go off stage, take some poison, and return as if nothing had happened, and then fall dead without a word at the feet of the man who was the cause of the whole affair. They asked, "How is the audience to know what killed her?" I had to say the obvious thing, "What else could an audience of intelligent theatregoers think when a woman goes out and comes back and dies without an explanation? That she had shot herself? That she had stabbed herself with a hairpin? The only inference is that she had poisoned herself." It was impossible for me to drive that into their heads.

What was the problem of the play? The problem was how to get the heroine through five acts and have her die in the last. It was a mighty difficult problem for me, you may be sure; but I solved it. I led her through all sorts of adventures, with a child at her heels, and her husband; and then, in the last act, as I have said, she saw it was impossible for her to continue, it being the fifth act, so she finished the matter by swallowing a dose of poison off stage.

I peddled that play about the Bowery until I got sick of life. I read it to friends, I read it to managers, until my vocal chords were ragged and frazzled. I read it to a group of players from the prompter's box in Herr Ritter's theatre. They sat around in the orchestra seats, and when I got through and looked around me the theatre was empty. I read it to Lecker, who is hard of hearing. I showed it to Kahn, telling him I had followed his directions, but he wouldn't let me read it. How many nights' sleep I lost trying to get Herr Burlak only to look at the manuscript!

Belvon, the husband of Madame Lessin, at that time set up as a manager by hiring a little theatre up the Bowery, and he got together a number of players from the provinces to support her. As soon as Fusher told me about the new venture, I went to Belvon with my play.

Now, do you know Belvon? Then you know what his reputation is; but I was so interested in my play that I forgot, as it were, who and what Belvon was. When he said he would produce my play, I fell on his neck and wept, before he could say another word. When he recovered from his surprise, he repeated that he would produce the play on one condition. His wife must approve of it also. Naturally, I said; so much the better. He rolled the manuscript into a bundle and took it to his wife. He then sent for me. I came into the little office of his theatre and was offered a chair, which was very nice of him—no?

"Madame Lessin is charmed with your play," said Belvon. "But there will have to be some fixing done. Do you object to fixings?"

I told him I objected to nothing, provided the play was produced with my name on it.

"You will understand," he continued, pleased with my reply, "that a play of this importance and worth costs lots of money to produce. There is the scenery, five large sets, all new; there is the extra music and the costumes; and then the chances that I take that it may be above the heads of the audience. You understand what the difficulties are?"

I said I understood everything. He looked at me with his sharp cat's eyes and handed me a cheap cigar, which I lit, and then sat down to listen to his proposal.

"That is a good play, generally speaking," he said. "You are a new author; you have no following. Is it right, I ask, that I, the manager, who have maybe fifty plays in my desk, should stand all the expense? No. I owe it to my theatre, to my wife, and to myself, not to speak of my partner, to ask you to stand some of the preliminary expenses. It will not amount to much, considering."

Although I knew my play was a good one, I was not unprepared for this proposition. I was cautious. I suspected what sort of customer I was dealing with; so I made bold to say that I must know exactly what the expenses would be, "considering" everything.

"You are right, you are right, Mr. Yachson," said Belvon. "You ought to know; so I will tell you. It will cost you, in round figures, three hundred dollars. Three hundred dollars, and I produce your play this season."

My cigar went out, and I laid it in the ashtray. I swallowed the lump in my throat, looked at him good and hard, and then said, "Under these conditions, you will produce it?"

"I give you my word of honor," he replied.

For his word of honor today I wouldn't give two cents.

I had two hundred dollars in the bank, hard-earned money in the waiting business. I withdrew it and went over to a cousin who lived in Brownsville and borrowed one hundred dollars from him, giving him my note for six months. I kept the whole matter a secret from my wife and friends, and the next day went over to the theatre and handed three hundred dollars in bills to Belvon.

Belvon looked at me astounded, probably because he did not believe I had so much faith in my own work; but after he had recovered from his astonishment he put the bills in his safe, gave me a receipt, and told me to come back again in a week.

I came again in a week. Belvon was nervous. But he greeted me cordially. He said that he was not going to announce my play until he saw how the new holiday piece took. He was sure that it would be withdrawn after the holidays; but he could not afford to confess that it was a failure until some time later. He told me to call again in ten days.

I called again in ten days. As he had predicted, the holiday piece was drawing poorly. A new play would have to be rehearsed soon. I saw that, and Belvon saw that I saw that. So he said to me, "Your play will be announced at the end of the week."

Sure enough, my play was announced. He had given it a new name; but that didn't bother me. My name was there as its author. The next day the East Side was in an uproar.

Everyone who came into Zeitlen's wanted to know the plot. I walked the streets like a hero. My wife stopped gallivanting about, and actually spoke respectfully to me. Patrons of Zeitlen's were curious to know a waiter who could write dramas. I was feeling hopeful for the future of the Yiddish drama, you may be sure.

I dreamed how my play was to be staged, and I imagined the jokes Badchen would interpolate in the play, and what fine words Burlak would give to the hero, and how Madame Lessin would, as the saying goes, chew the ground when she played the heroine. I heard the applause of the gallery gods, my friends. An article was written about me in the newspapers. How's this, a dramatist-waiter? Something new under the sun! Finally Zeitlen gave me orders not to speak to the customers about my play; he didn't like it. So there I was for a time like a volcano strangling before an eruption, as it were. You understand?

What was my amazement a week later, on a Monday morning, to see posters in the windows announcing that the next play at Lessin's theatre was to be a domestic drama by Krolik!

I rushed over to Belvon's office like crazy, and went in to see him without waiting to be invited. He was there with that timid little Krolik. Filled with mortification and anger, I shouted:

"What does this mean? What has become of 'The Sins of the Mothers'? How is this? You announce a new play by Krolik! This is outrageous! This is terrible! Explain, explain, explain!"

Belvon was a bit flustered by my sudden appearance, and Krolik, true to his character, slunk out of the office. At first Belvon tried to calm me, to pacify me. When I am angry, I am terrifying. Finally, after I became composed, Belvon said:

"Don't put the blame on me. Blame those rotten actors and their union."

"What do you mean?" I shouted.

"There are three men fighting for one part, and not one will give way. Rosenstein and Crohn and Mordecai swear that the leading part belongs to each one of them. Rosenstein will not play, Crohn will not play, Mordecai will not play unless it's the leading part. So what shall I do?"

"Who's the boss?" I asked indignantly.

"The boss is the union," said Belvon. "According to the rules, an actor cannot be forced to play a part not in his line or in his class. The part you have there for the husband is the only part the three leading men I have can play. If they refuse to play any other part, I can't play the drama, excellent as it is."

I was overwhelmed. In vain I flourished my contract in his face. Belvon shrugged his shoulders and shouted back at me:

"See the union!"

Like a madman I went over to see Rosenstein. I implored him to give the part to Mordecai and to play something else. Do you know him? He has shifting eyes; he is so conceited that nobody can tolerate him. He was jealous of Mordecai, and not for the world would he give way to him, he said.

I ran over to that moon-faced Crohn, whose imbecile look I have always detested. He would not resign in Mordecai's favor because he had just married and did not want his wife to think he was a second-class actor.

When I saw Mordecai, who is the best actor of the three, he said he did not believe in having dramatists interfere with the casting of their plays. That was his excuse.

In despair, I went to the union and laid my case before them in open meeting. All of them knew me and sympathized with me; but in this matter they acted on union principles. It was the artist's prerogative not to play anything he did not want to play. They would not let Belvon cast the part.

Then I organized a meeting to protest against the union; but when I went to hire the hall I could not get one, nor could I get any speakers to condemn the union. There wasn't a newspaper to print a line about the affair. You have to have some nerve to stand against the union.

I saw it was no use fighting Fate; so I decided to see Belvon and get my money back; I said to him:

"You are not going to produce my play, I can see that. But my money—my three hundred dollars?"

He put his hands in his pockets, looked at me, and laughed out loud. "Your three hundred dollars!" he said. "What have I to do with it? Take back your play and the rubbish I bought for scenery and costumes and do what you please with it. You've got a nerve to ask me for money! I have invested in your play three times three hundred dollars, and if you were an honest man, so help me God, you would pay what I lost, not to speak at all of the three hundred!"

"Then I owe you money besides?" I exclaimed.

"You certainly do!" he replied. "But we'll call it quits, and that settles the business."

"But I don't call this quits!" I shouted. "I'll sue you! I'll blacken your name in the papers! I'll not let up until I get my money back!"

"If that's the sort of customer you are," said Belvon, turning pale and red, "take your play and get right out of here!"

He called in his bouncer, you understand, who kicked me out of the office, throwing the manuscript of my play after me. I picked up the manuscript and myself and went to the restaurant.

The long and short of it is, I didn't sue him, I didn't blacken his name in the papers, and I didn't get my three hundred dollars back.

Misfortune seemed to follow me. I was taboo with every manager. Within three weeks after Belvon kicked me out my wife left me, and Zeitlen gave me notice to quit, and when the one-hundred dollar note came round I had to pay with my sweat. Luckily Shullem gave me a job, and here I am, without courage or hope, ashamed to look my former friends in the face, and with no ambition in life.

All because Belvon swindled me, and banged the door on my ambition for three hundred dollars. For, as you may have surmised, if you know anything of the Yiddish theatre, the three actors, who were dying to play the one part in my play, were put up to it by Belvon himself, and his eye all the while was not on my future but on my hard-earned dollars.

A few days ago who do I meet in the street but Belvon, wearing a heavy fur overcoat and smoking a cigar with a gold band around it.

I said, "Hello, scoundrel!"

He says: "Hello, dramatic genius!"

I say, "What about my three hundred dollars?"

He says: "You idiot, are you still kicking about that? Don't you know that you ought to consider me your bene-factor?"

I say, "May you live to see next season, if you are not a liar!"

He says, "What have you lost? Three hundred dollars. What have you gained, though? You've gained this: people still think, maybe—you can never tell—the play that wasn't

played might have been a good one. But if the play had
been produced, what would they have said of you? You
know what. A rotten play, that's all. A rotten dramatist,
who shouldn't have been let within six hundred feet of a
theatre, and that's all. Who made this possible, who's your
benefactor? Belvon, and that's all!"

Well, what was I to say to that?

What do *you* say to that? Belvon's my benefactor, that's
all!

XIV

Out into the Great World

BURLAK, THE ONLY ACTOR RITTER REGARDED AS HIS RIVAL, HAD reached the end of his rope. He was now looking back at his past. There was nothing to look forward to. When the cup of stage glory is filled to the brim, one naturally takes stock, settles down to reflection and arrives at a "philosophy of life." What is called philosophy is the explanation the weary traveler gives of his mood. It is the defense of all he had done in his life. Burlak was settling down.

Behold Burlak—bull-necked, bull-voiced, with round head, thick lips, red face, bulging chest; the idol of all those who would not have Ritter as their king; an actor of varied parts, in all of which the Burlak label stuck out conspicuously; now in his fiftieth year, sighing for new worlds to conquer, but not a new world in sight. He had spent his entire life among his own people, a stiff-necked people, easily pleased, easily angered, easily bluffed, loyal but volatile. He had never known the pain of a thorough critical trouncing. He had not known the meaning of the word "broke," and yet his soul was not satisfied.

"I am an actor-artist," he said in Marcus's café. "Do you suppose that I, the finest Othello on the Yiddish stage, like to play in Lecker's 'She Wanted a Husband'? Every time I play in one of those *shund* plays my heart is lacerated and bleeds. High ideals on the Yiddish stage is impossible. You know what I mean. You got to be a Stoic to carry on. Only my philosophy enables me to bear up under it, and so I play on!"

For twenty years Burlak had been a Stoic, and reaped a golden harvest. And he remained a Stoic until a special benefit was given for the great dramatist Manewitz, in his theatre, sponsored by two hundred uptown intellectuals who had been corralled into the theatre by Schiffman, an enterprising friend of the beneficiary, a sophomore at Columbia, who pretended that in Manewitz he had discovered the Yiddish Ibsen.

A Yiddish benefit has its own definition. In the Broadway theatre a benefit is given for one who is broke. An actor or manager or press agent becomes destitute; a benefit is arranged to rehabilitate him. On the Yiddish stage a benefit is exactly what is stated, nothing more. It is a performance for the benefit of some person who is not stone broke, is not incapacitated, and who is, on the contrary, the chief agent in the sale of the tickets. He runs a benefit for himself.

The Manewitz benefit was for the benefit of Manewitz, who at that time sorely needed the money, but it was arranged by Schiffman. The two hundred professors and professional men Schiffman invited were expected to pay for their seats by liberal appreciations in the form of disserta-

tions on the dramaturgical ability of Manewitz. That was
worth something for its indirect influence on the East Side,
but Manewitz's personal interest was centered in the gate
receipts.

It was a matinee performance. Burlak had the leading
role. He saw before him a mixed audience, three or four
rows of sedate professors, settlement workers, artists, literary men, all sitting quietly. The East Side intelligentsia
were given seats a little to the rear; they would not be gotten to stay away; they were determined to mingle with
the élite of the Gentile world. The three or four rows of
outsiders were like bands of gold in the audience, and Burlak, as he played, felt that when they applauded it sounded
better than a Tchaikowsky symphony. He played with fervor. He felt that he had been playing all his life to primitive,
raw, uncouth, awkward people. The world he had been
playing in seemed walled off from the outer world, and the
sounds of his acting reverberated loudly. It was like coming into the metropolis after a severe winter in the provinces. It was like coming into the presence of culture after
having lived among savages.

Burlak was married, and strange to say, happily married,
for his wife was not an actress. Some years ago Burlak had
induced her to leave her well-to-do husband, who was a
merchant on the East Side. She had fallen in love with the
actor and left home, luxury, and children, to follow him.
When she obtained her divorce, Burlak had married her
and lived happily ever after—which upsets, quite, all standards of morality. Madame Burlak was just touched by
knowledge of the world outside the Ghetto. She had always
longed for her husband to be distinguished, anywhere. But
she knew too little of that outer world, so she always kept
her longing to herself. As an admirer of Burlak's acting,

she was worth a regiment of patriots. She was full of life, and, what was worth more, she was an excellent cook. To appreciate her cooking, one should get a look at Burlak in tights; he was her finest exhibit.

Madame Burlak came into his dressing-room after the Manewitz performance and kissed him with fervor.

"That was a great audience," she said, "and how they appreciated your playing!"

"What have I always told you? Moshe remains Moshe, no matter what our socialist friends may say," exclaimed Burlak, while his dresser jerked at his boots. "They have the taste of soldiers in barracks. Now, take these professors, these literature men, they know what art is. They may not understand the language, but human nature they know. And what drama is any good if it can't be understood by any one, language or no language? Ah, give me audiences like this, and I could play——"

He was praised by Prof. Brindle Jones, the erudite note-maker on the French drama; James Bronson Garrison, a settlement worker, who had seen the Passion Play and spent a season in Paris, and who declared that Burlak's acting astounded him! Burlak bowed in acknowledgment of the compliment. A gentleman who had written a drama which was so indecent that no New York manager was sufficiently advanced to produce it declared that he would dedicate his next play to Burlak. Schiffman, running in and out of the admiring groups, shook Burlak's hands warmly and said:

"You can't tell what will come of this, Mr. Burlak."

Burlak went home with his beaming wife, and in the privacy of his home burst the bonds that held his soul in fetters, and dared give utterance to his ambition.

"Enough, enough, dear Isabella!" he exclaimed, pacing up and down the room. "Too long have I wasted my talent on this desert of ignorance! Too long have I played to please the inexperienced, poverty-stricken proletarian intelligentsia of this quarter. I have been throwing pearls before swine. I have been creating masterpieces of art for the blind. I have been singing my heart out to those who are tone-deaf. Let me get out of this stifling atmosphere! Let me get into that pure realm of art, where millions may applaud, where culture is evenly distributed, where, when they say good, that settles it."

Isabella listened with admiration. She stroked his curly head and patted his cheek.

"And what are you going to do, my dear?" she asked softly.

"I shall tell the Yiddish stage to go to hell," he said.

"First, I must have a play. Who shall write it for me?" mused Burlak.

He had his wife invite Schiffman for supper. Schiffman, always eager to extend the circle of his influence, arrived in a suit of clothes that was the pink of fashion, with beautiful patent-leather shoes, and twirled a thin, serpentine cane.

He ate his dinner, his ears burning with impatience, and after cigars were lit, Burlak said:

"I have decided to go upon the American stage."

"You don't say!" Schiffman exclaimed.

"Yes, I do say," repeated Burlak, chewing his cigar savagely.

"That's what I've been saying too," said Schiffman, recovering from his astonishment. "Only last week I told Manewitz that you were the one actor among us to take on the American stage. Your manner, your voice, your temperament, you know."

"Exactly, my temperament," said Burlak. "The English

language I know well enough. I can talk with the best of
them. My pronunciation ain't so good, but a few weeks'
training will put that right, and there you are."

"What will you play, Mr. Burlak?" asked Schiffman,
timidly.

"That is what I want to see you about," said Burlak.
"You are acquainted with the professors. Can't you find out
whether one of them hasn't got a play that would suit me?"

"I know Professor Jones very well," said Schiffman, "and
then there's Algernon Tingley, who has many problem
plays; but what kind of a play would you like?"

"Well, you know what I mean, my dear Schiffman," said
Burlak. "I needn't tell you. You seen me play all my repertoire. You understand what I mean, you know. Let them
give me something like Manewitz' 'Wahrheit,' where I play
an American, with some emotional scenes, strong plot, good
juicy dialogue. What's the use of talking? You know what
I mean."

"You know what I mean" was one of Burlak's insinuating
phrases. Schiffman was no novice, and he knew what Burlak meant. He wrinkled his brow, scratched his ear, walked
up and down the room, and finally said:

"Why do you need to look all over New York for a play?
I have a play that has in it all that you mean and more.
It has a scene stronger than the one in the 'Wahrheit,' more
powerful than the one in 'The Slaughter,' more effective
than the one in 'The Charlatan.' I made that play specially
for you."

"You wrote it? My dear Schiffman!" exclaimed Burlak,
rushing to him with outstretched arms. "If you have written a play just as you say, then why should I look further?
You and me—you know what I mean—we can fix it up, and
then there can be no doubt of its being fit."

"When should I come up and read it?" asked Schiffman eagerly.

"We'll take a few days off at Lakewood, and you'll read me your play from beginning to end," said Burlak.

He was delighted. The play had in it, as Schiffman had suggested, scenes of a number of his well-known successes. There was dialogue he could "chew up the carpet" with. It was exactly fitted to him. With Schiffman he went to a Broadway manager and discussed a business proposition. He would finance his own production. All he wanted was the services of a firm to direct the tour. A little, dissipated occupant of an imposing desk made the arrangements. He placed at Burlak's disposal one of his ablest stage managers. Burlak gave him a check and a press agent was at once set to work.

The news spread like wildfire over the East Side. Their Burlak was about to leave them! The man who had entertained them for years, who had grown up with them, who had received all he had from them, was to desert them. The clamor of many voices was heard in the Yiddish press. They realized at once what would be their loss when Burlak left them. The somnolent critics, who often wrote their play reviews in serial installments, initiated discussions on the decay of the Yiddish stage. Some of them were proud of the honor implied by Burlak's desertion. One black-haired critic with an enormous high brow saw in this desertion proof of the cosmopolitan value of Yiddish acting.

No one doubted that Burlak would at once take his place among the stars of the first magnitude. His talent, his voice, his deportment—he would rank with Coquelin, with Mansfield. Should he appear in "Hamlet," he would be compared

with Edwin Booth, and not to his disadvantage. Salvini's
Othello would come down a peg.

A sadness mingled with justifiable vanity came over Burlak. He was tearing himself away from his native soil. As
he was about to depart he was reminded everywhere of the
greatness of his local fame, and his gratitude had in it a
touch of that feeling every man thinking of his own death
feels toward those who, he knows, will speak a good word at
his grave. One evening Burlak was called before the curtain, the applause was tumultuous, and he was compelled
to make a speech.

"You have heard that this fall I leave you," he said, feeling for his words, "but when I go away I shall always
remember your loyalty, and appreciate your appreciation,
and—and—and you know what I mean, my friends, you
know what I mean."

They really did not know what he meant, but they saw
that a lump had risen in his throat which prevented him
from telling it.

Burlak and Schiffman proceeded with the rehearsals. In
order to make his transition to the American stage easier
Burlak was to play a Jew with American manners. The
stage manager was a bow-legged Irish lad, who was familiar
with all sorts of productions, and having been given carte
blanche in the direction of this new enterprise, he set to
work with energy. He had nothing to lose.

What he did to Schiffman's play deserves to be recorded
in the annals of a slaughterhouse. There were good, thick
speeches that Burlak had read with gusto. When the first
rehearsal was held all these speeches were lost, and there
was none to account for their disappearance. Schiffman
stood by with a pale face, seeking to prevent the bloodthirsty
manager from wielding his ax (alias blue-pencil), but it

was done with such lightning-like rapidity that he had only to turn his back for a few minutes and long stretches of dialogue would disappear. And he had been so proud of his dialogue!

Burlak was kept in a tumult of agitation. He had learned his part by heart, an unusual thing for him, but during the rehearsals every one of his words was amputated or transformed to a degree which made it necessary after each rehearsal to recommit his part to memory. There were whole scenes transposed. The characters were baptized without mercy by the stage manager. The Jewish milieu was abandoned and a mongrel Presbyterian and Catholic atmosphere was introduced. The Jewish lad became an Irish lad. Speeches intended for Burlak was given to the heroine or the heroine's father. In a word, Schiffman's drama was whipped into shape with a great deal of squealing and groaning.

Burlak took lunch with Schiffman one afternoon and confided in him.

"Do you think that O'Reilly knows his business?" he asked.

Schiffman looked around cautiously. It was his first play; his first chance for a metropolitan production.

"Don't speak loud," he replied. "But between you and me if ever there was a butcher, an ignoramus that doesn't know literature when he sees it, it's that fellow. My God! What has he done with my touching effect in the third act? What has he done with my fine lines? Where have they gone to?"

"But what is there to be done?" asked Burlak. "You—you know what I mean. What shall I do about it? If the play is turned into a machine-made play what's the good? Will it pay me to make a failure? You know what I mean, my dear fellow."

"Don't be afraid," replied Schiffman. "For your purposes it may come out better, because as I wrote it, it was a fine literary play. What they are doing to it is to turn it into a popular, successful, good-for-nothing American play. You need say nothing, but it's me, my artistic ideals, my ambitions that will suffer."

"Is that all? Then if it becomes a successful play you'll draw your royalties, so why should you care?" said Burlak, relieved.

"But what will the Columbia professors think of me?" said Schiffman sadly.

Mme. Burlak came regularly to the rehearsals. She saw her husband ordered about, heard him take directions from O'Reilly, and felt ashamed that he, the great star, should be treated so shabbily by the manager. But she was consoled when she saw Burlak falling into line with the other players, speaking English that to her ears was so musical, and she was glad.

They tried it out in some New England city, where a Stoic hardness was characteristic of the audience. What that dog-town said did not matter. They were coming into New York via Boston, the seat of culture, unadulterated by alienisms. Their advent in Boston was hailed by the notables of the dramatic columns with pompous and serious comment. The history of every foreign actor who had become an American player was given in detail. The critics awaited the debut of Burlak with impatience. The event was to be a dramatic treat.

Harbingers of good tidings came to New York at once with the good tidings. Schiffman was the first. He announced with a swagger, "Success!" He had with him clippings of all the Boston newspapers. Columns were devoted to an analysis of the acting of the great Yiddish actor. One writer dissected his playing act by act, consuming the greater part of his vocabulary in adjectives that made precise distinctions. The play was subjected to the same rigorous treatment. The conclusion was—a great, potent force, an actor of great possibilities, a play of virile interest, worthy, however, of deeper study. The deeper study, however, consumed so much time that Burlak was on his way to New York before the articles born of study were written.

The Yiddish press, elated, printed every word of favorable comment. Burlak's pictures adorned every story. The East Side girded its loins and proceeded to the Broadway theatre, where he was to make his first appearance in New York.

"I shall go to the theatre," said Dahlman to Fusher, "and I shall hoot him off the stage."

"Insane!" exclaimed Fusher. "What do you mean? You'll go and hoot the great Burlak off the stage?"

"When a man is about to make a damn fool of himself before *goyim,* it's the business of us Jews to repudiate him," said Dahlman.

Dahlman went alone to the theatre.

From orchestra to gallery the edifice was packed with an East Side crowd. The dramatic critics examined the audience thoroughly before the curtain was rung up and declared that it was more interesting than the play possibly could be.

In the wings stood Madame Burlak, Schiffman, and several of their personal friends. The great Burlak was in a terrible perspiration. He constantly looked through the peephole at the audience and glanced at his wife.

The curtain arose, and the entrance of the star was greeted with showers of flowers, prolonged applause, and cheers. Mme. Burlak had seen to this. Dahlman sat in his seat unconcerned; the critics likewise. The play proceeded. Burlak went through his part with animation, with an incessant movement of his hands. He was constantly alive. He could not remain in repose. He acted with great energy after the curtain and was compelled to bow five times. Crowds of his friends rushed to the stage to congratulate him. He received them with a smile, triumphant. Belvon, the husband of Mme. Lessin, took him aside and said:

"You fool—reserve your strength for the last act."

The third act received a well-directed salvo of applause, with insistent demands that Burlak make a speech, which he at once proceeded to do. He was visibly embarrassed, but succeeded in making himself heard to this extent:

"*Meine Herren und Damen*—you know what I mean—ladies and gentlemen—I don't know what to say, but when a man—if—and—you know what I mean—thank you." It was a brilliant effort.

After the performance a banquet was given by Mme. Burlak to a number of her husband's friends at the Café Boulevard. Burlak received innumerable congratulations.

"Have you seen what the Boston papers said of me?" he asked Kahn, the editor of the radical Yiddish daily.

"We also printed it," replied Kahn, with a smile.

"*There* are critics for you, in Boston!" said Burlak.

The next morning Burlak awoke with a headache. He rushed out of bed and called for the morning papers. His wife read the reviews to him.

It was quite apparent that New York was far behind Boston in culture and appreciation of playing. That was not to be wondered at. Over in Boston the intellectuality of the community is more evenly distributed. Life is simpler, there are fewer of the conflicts of ideals, there is less of bustle and ferment, the influence of those teachers of culture and conduct like Emerson and Thoreau and Alcott is so pervasive that appreciation of dramatic art is more highly developed. It has more naïveté because of its bookishness. It is highbrow with a literary background. New York is just helter-skelter. It has no set standards. It is a sort of hostel into which all are invited. Its tone is set by the last newcomer. It is an all-year-round Coney Island. Therefore, what Boston said was white, New York said was rotten. The things Boston admired, New York ridiculed. Boston said Burlak had talent. New York said Burlak had big feet. Boston said Burlak had temperament. New York said that he had too many hands.

Burlak asked his wife to stop reading.

"To hell with New York! The Boston critics are right," he stormed.

"And I thought they were so interested," said Mme. Burlak.

"They are a set of grafters," said Burlak. "If I had only greased their palms, I suppose they would have had other eyes. I was told about this, but shall I so degrade myself as to bribe a critic? Not in a million years. We'll show them. The people will come to see me, and their criticisms will count for nothing."

Schiffman rushed into the house, his pockets bulging with newspapers. He was in a great rage. His face was pale. He flourished the papers as he entered.

"Do you see what they say of my play?" he shouted.

The fact was, Burlak had not thought of the play at all.

"They say that the third act is full of incongruities," exclaimed Schiffman, dancing about the room. "They say that the scene in the second act, where you go to the phone, was a mistake; Blakely should have gone to the phone. They say that the dialogue is insipid, the characters grotesque, the situations contrived. Contrived, as if any situation on the stage were not contrived! And—and—do you see what you and O'Reilly have done to my play? You have distorted it beyond recognition. You have spoiled my first play. You have made me a laughingstock wherever I go. I'm not going to stand for this!"

"What can you do about it? See what they say about me," said Burlak, accompanying Schiffman in his mad gyrations about the floor.

"Yes, read what they say of Herr Burlak," his wife said.

"What they say of you I don't care," declared Schiffman. "But they are not going to treat me like this. I'm not going to keep quiet."

"What will you do?" she asked.

"I'm going to tell the newspapers just what you and O'Reilly did to my play," said Schiffman furiously. "I shall repudiate it altogether. It isn't mine. You changed the characters. You left out whole scenes. You put in words I never wrote. I shall tell that to the newspapers, and then see what happens."

"If you do that you won't get any royalties, let me tell you," said Burlak.

"What do I care for royalties? My reputation! My reputation!" shouted Schiffman.

"Let us go together to see O'Reilly," said Burlak.

They went over to the theatre and found O'Reilly on the stage. O'Reilly, with a broad grin, greeted them first.

"Well, they haven't done a thing to you, have they?" he said.

"But you saw what they said in Boston," insisted Burlak.

"Oh, those highbrows in Boston are punk," declared O'Reilly. "They are so stuck on themselves that when an

opening comes they take it as a gift from heaven. It's their
business to let you down easy, but they smother it with
words, and you don't know it. The boys in this town know
their business."

Burlak took Schiffman aside and had an earnest conversation with him.

"If you make this fuss in the papers, Schiffman," he
said, "then it is all up with us. You know what I mean.
We won't be able to show our faces. Now, be a good boy
and say nothing. This will blow over, and we can play in
New York at least for a month, and you'll be getting royalties. Roasting is good for a playwright; it's rotten only for
an actor."

Schiffman allowed himself to be persuaded. He stifled
his conscience in the prospect of royalties.

But very little of his conscience was destined to be stifled.
The audiences began to dwindle. The third night the press
agent found it difficult to fill the orchestra seats. The fourth
night there was a deserted house. Friday night the house
was again filled with curious East Siders, and the same
thing happened on Saturday afternoon and Saturday evening. On Monday evening the house was deserted, about two
hundred deadheads yawning in front of the curtain. On
Tuesday evening Burlak's heart was heavy as he looked out
and saw rows upon rows of empty benches. But he had to
play his two weeks. He could not wind up in the middle of
the week. That same evening Belvon came into Burlak's
dressing-room after a silent curtain on the third act, and
said to the discouraged player:

"You *podletz*, you miserable good-for-nothing, what are
you doing here on Broadway? Go back home, you scoundrel!"

And he at once made an offer to Burlak to appear the

following week with Madame Lessin in a special three weeks' star engagement. Burlak accepted it on the spot.

"They ain't worth wasting time on," said Burlak.

Years later, Burlak looked at things philosophically, like the Stoic he was.

"Where an artist plays is not important," he said. "Art shines through walls of ignorance. It rises through the mire. In Boston it was easier; in New York it could not break through. There they have culture, thick. Here, what have you got? Just a thick wall of ignorant trash! They don't know what art means."

XV

Mr. Ritter and Shylock

IN THE EARLY DAYS, WHEN RITTER GAVE A PLAY WITH SOCIALIST
tendencies, he became aware of the class-struggle and used
the stage—between the acts—as his soap-box. He was just as
sensitive, however, to propaganda of a different kind. When
a former radical spat at internationalism and wrote a play
in praise of the hills of Zion, Ritter had a picture of Theo-
dor Herzl rigged up in the lobby and entertained his audiences with sentimental Zionist observations. He changed
his convictions with his plays. He was easily persuaded by
his own impersonations.

There are actors who cannot get rid of the stage when
they leave it. The grease paint gets into their ears. The
rouge cannot be washed away. The words of their parts per-
sist in their off-stage conversation. Their gestures and manner of speaking become fixed habit. You can spot them at
once as they swagger into Marcus's coffee-house, waving
their hands, haranguing one another in their mimicry of

German—the ideal language of theatrical bombast. They use few words of their own. They have no ideas of their own. They quote the sentiments of the hero or villain, or the jests of the comedian. Behind the impersonation there sticks out, at times, a peasant, a tailor, a blacksmith, or a pickpocket, but they seldom unmask themselves.

Years ago, when Ritter strolled into the theatre as a callow youth, he had been a clerk in a haberdashery in Odessa. He was an indifferent player, and gave little promise of ability. He lived more off the stage than on it. His interest was not in the theatre, but the life around it. He played with actors (and mocked them), ate with them and slept with them; but when the vagabond period was over, all of them (with few exceptions) settled down. The nomadic spirit was stilled. And even Ritter, the wildest of them all, became the slave of routine. He even allowed himself to be married, and when Dikman relieved him of his wife he married again, appropriating the wife of a second-rate comedian and rearing a large and varied family of children. After he had eased Dikman into the limbo of obscurity, he became the first star-manager in New York. But he was not allowed to hold that eminence alone. Out of the dust of rivalry eventually two stars of the first magnitude were born.

Ritter's rival was Burlak, who spluttered his way to the front row of actors. There was something cheerful and dependable about Burlak. He was sturdy and vain, and could laugh heartily. He began as a singer in Odessa. He was the first Absalom in Goldfaden's "Shulamith." Then his voice became bullish and he had to find other parts in which singing was incidental, and singing off-key was licensed. (After all, they were not playing grand opera.) He was younger than Ritter. His hair was a dark brown, and Ritter's was silver white. They should have lived side by side in peace, for Burlak found his métier in romantic plays, and Ritter was a specialist in character parts. But they could not avoid collision, for they had their own patriots who carried on the fight for them. The gallery gods of the one had to boo the playing of the other; and often parties were organized to tear down the playing of the rival of their idol.

Well, let's open the door and have Fusher come in. (He's been waiting long enough.)

How can I bar the way to Mr. Fusher? Goulash debated. Journalists had certain rights, and they were often allowed in Mr. Ritter's dressing-room; but could it be said that Mr. Fusher was a journalist? He was the discoverer of Manewitz, and that gave him a status. He was often seen with actors and journalists on the street and in the coffee-houses. But while Goulash was debating the matter, Fusher pushed his way into Ritter's dressing-room, and Goulash rushed after him, standing behind him, protesting to Ritter, apologizing for the intrusion.

"This is impudence, Mr. Fusher," said Ritter, "Get the hell right out of here."

"When you hear the news, you'll thank me," said Fusher, reaching for the cigarettes.

"What news?" asked Ritter.

"It's Burlak," said Fusher. "He threatens to play Hamlet."

"That's none of my concern," said Ritter. "I have gone beyond Shakespeare, and I'll never go back to him. Let Burlak stick in the mud, if he likes it."

"No great actor can run away from Shakespeare," said Fusher. "He is the actor's playwright. Only in the gallery of his plays can an actor match his art against four hundred years of the theatre. Don't pretend Burlak doesn't interest

you. When he plays Hamlet, he qualifies as a classical tragedian. Then, what happens to Ritter? Good night to you;
good morning to Burlak."

Ritter looked up.

"What are you thinking of?" he asked.

"It's fate and destiny," said Fusher. "you've got to play
Shylock. In that play you challenge comparison with Possart
and Sonnenthal and Henry Irving. I have a young man
who has translated and adapted it. A fine young poet. His
name is Dahlman. You've heard of him. Say the word and
he'll come to explain what he's got."

Ritter thought it would cost him nothing to say the word,
so he said it.

Dahlman was a daring fellow who played the part of
Villon, the vagabond poet, in the coffee-houses and club-
rooms. That is, he was a slovenly, disreputable vagabond
and scamp. He wrote proletarian poetry. One of his poems
had been set to music and was sung at radical meetings. He
declaimed his own verse to a coterie in a Rumanian wine-
cellar. He also translated wicked French stories and sold
them to the radical press. He often spoke of plays he was
writing, discussed them, recited from them, but never produced the manuscripts although managers on occasion were
known to have suggested business talks. He was always
talking about himself, and while he was talking, was voted
an interesting fellow, but when he left, it was the general
opinion that he was a bore.

Dahlman made his way to Ritter's home on 4th Street,
and stood in the stuffy parlor for fully an hour before Ritter made his appearance. He was dressed in a red robe
with a yellow silk lining. This was the informal dress of
every star at the time. It was the undress uniform of the
actor who had really made good. It would have been a

breach of etiquette to wear anything else while lolling about the house or making-up in the dressing-room.

When Ritter offered cigarettes, Dahlman looked at him boldly. That look meant to say: I am a poet and you are a clod. I am the immortal, you are the passing moment. I am the star, you are the dust.

"What can I do for you?" said Ritter.

"You mean what I can do for you," said Dahlman, scowling.

"I hate arguing after breakfast," said Ritter. "Sit down, and tell me what you've got."

"I've got the play I've made of 'The Merchant of Venice,' said Dahlman.

"So you want to sell me Shakespeare's Shylock," said Ritter, laughing. "What about the Woolworth Building?"

"Don't be so crude," said Dahlman. "I sell only that which is my own. First, I have translated 'The Merchant of Venice'—for the first time—into the finest Yiddish of all times. Second, I have given it a modern adaptation. I have made it sound and look as if it were written yesterday. It's fresh; it's unconventional."

Dahlman produced the manuscript and fingered the pages.

"Shall I begin?" he queried.

"For God's sake—no!" exclaimed Ritter. "I won't have it read it to me—under no circumstances. What I want to know, what are you selling—Shakespeare or Dahlman?"

"I'll say fifty-fifty," Dahlman admitted. "It'll bring Shakespeare back to life."

Ritter took the play and promised to let him know as soon as possible, and hustled Dahlman out of the house.

It was the first time the suggestion had been made to Ritter that he play Shylock. But he hated declamation and the classical, for he could not play according to any tradi-

tion. He was an actor who made his own style. He could
build up a character as Richard Mansfield did in "A Pari-
sian Romance"; and through make-up and detail and
emphasis, make it appear real. That was what kept him in
the lower ranks in the early days in Odessa and in London.
He was incapable of carrying a tune. He was not agile on
his legs. In the plays of Goldfaden and those who imitated
the old maestro, there were no parts in which he personally
could distinguish himself. Only when he was given an un-
worked-out part in an indifferent play which he could build
up was it possible for him to be recognized as a superior
player.

Nor had he ever read Shakespeare. He could not read
German, and there were few Yiddish translations. When he
read Dahlman's manuscript, it was his first experience with
the text of the play. He knew the traditions of Shylock from
hearsay. He remembered Possart playing it in the Irving
Place Theatre, but he had not seen it. "The Merchant of
Venice" as a play to be played, in its entirety, he had never
encountered. And here it was written in a Yiddish he could
understand.

When he decided to play it (chiefly to spite Burlak), he
gave Dahlman a few hundred dollars. "That will hold the
scamp," he thought. He discussed with him how he intended
to play the part, and to his surprise found Dahlman strongly
opposed to his plans.

Ritter was thinking of playing Shylock in a vein of protest, but softly. He thought that he could use that interpre-
tation to win the sympathy of Jews. He did not want to
rail. He did not want to appear hard-hearted, but he would
find ways to express an iron will under a mild exterior.

"Don't be a fool," said Dahlman. "You have to play Shylock the way Shakespeare wrote it. He wanted the Jew to

be vindictive. He wanted him to be hated and to be defeated and derided in the end. You've got to play him that way, and if you don't, even the Jewish audience will be disappointed. They enjoy the tragedy of Shylock. Their own sufferings are reflected in his. Their own protest is expressed in his bitter raillery."

"You are wrong, and I'm going to prove it to you," said Ritter. He felt that he could not play Shylock unless he was made the symbol of a cause. There was the ancient grudge born of persecution. He stood for justice and law. He exposed the hypocrisy of the Christians in the play.

Strange to say, however, whatever Ritter thought of the symbol, what he showed on the stage was the same old Shylock, almost in the manner of Henry Irving. He was a great success. He made a splendid figure—a Sephardic Jew, black-bearded, arrogant, ingratiating, and vindictive. He was indeed the symbol of a persecuted and despised race, turning upon his persecutors.

A writer of books on the Ghetto of the East Side invited a group of Boston friends to go slumming with him. They dined at Lorber's, which was then on Grand Street. He suggested that they see Ritter as Shylock. They were taken to see him after the performance in his dressing-room. They saw him in his red dressing robe. He looked like a Roman senator. His voice was resonant, his manner was majestic, his gestures were graceful.

"What is your idea of Shylock?" the slum expert asked.

Ritter wound his dressing robe about his tall figure, placed his fingers lightly on the throne-chair which he always used in his dressing-room, and said:

"Shylock has been grossly misunderstood down to this day. He is Shakespeare's defense of the Jew. He uses the prejudices of the day as the setting and makes Shylock ex-

press the everlasting protest of Jews against the prejudices
that encircle them. The pound of flesh is an incident in the
story which Shakespeare disdained to eliminate. It was an
integral part of the plot. But even accepting the story, the
defense is a masterly work of art. Shylock vindicated his
people. He shows himself generous and courageous. His
memory of the ancient wrong is not personal. It relates to
his people. And how beautifully he exposes the hypocrisy
of his enemies! It is my hope that through playing Shylock
I shall raise the prestige of my people and contribute to
tolerance and goodwill. That is my hope."

They were impressed by his eloquence, but Dahlman
said that Ritter was deceiving himself. There were two
Shylocks struggling for mastery in him. There was the
Shylock he played, and the Shylock he loved to describe in
his between-the-act speeches. He thought he was making a
new figure of Shylock, but it was the traditional Jew with
a slightly different emphasis. In the end, Ritter himself
was poisoned by the Shylock he had set out to destroy. He
was unable to escape the fascinating influence of the Eliza-
bethan Shylock who represented avarice and greed.

In the olden days, Ritter ranted between the acts on
various subjects. That was make-believe. When he came to
Shylock he maintained the pose of defender of the prestige
of the Jew. That was impersonation.

An actor plays a wide range of parts before he finds himself. He may find himself in Hamlet, and all other roles
stem from it. He may fill the picture of a burly Macbeth,
and you have a wide range of fat parts to play in the repertoire of all theatres. Crook-backed Richard III may be just
the mould for you, and villains become your lot. When an
actor finds his métier, all his experience is poured into the
part that reflects him best, and there is nothing more to

be added. With the playing of Shylock, the blood in Ritter's veins was calmed. He had found himself.

As season followed season, and Ritter's Shylock known on Broadway, the coterie that adored him as an actor began to be disturbed about him as a person. He was hard with money and was loath to allow his dollars free circulation, as had once been his habit. They were astounded when he eased himself out of his contract with Dahlman and refused to pay him any more royalties. "What!" he exclaimed, "am I to pay that lousy poet royalties on a play Shakespeare wrote and I made famous?" When a committee-in-aid came and told him that Dahlman would have to be sent away to a sanatorium—"a little touched in the head"—he compromised by giving them a hundred dollars, with the understanding that it must be regarded as satisfaction in full.

He developed an obsession about trade unions, specifically the unions in the theatre. It became a matter of principle. He haggled about the wages. He saw no reason why the union should prescribe the number of employees he should engage—actors, ushers, musicians, scene-shifters, and chorus people. He wrote letters to the press, denouncing the unions as the oppressors of art, and protesting against tyranny.

He was always quarreling with his cashier, and hauled him over the coals for his "overhead." "Whatever he cannot explain," Ritter shouted, "he calls overhead. Keep the expense down, I tell you!" He discharged Zhilik, his dresser, and refused to give him compensation. "Why should he complain? For twenty years he has drawn regular wages. He should have gotten himself an annuity." He began to hoard money in secret, not telling his wife. She knew nothing of his bank account uptown. This enabled him to plead a shortage of funds whenever she was in an extravagant mood.

And then, what was even more disturbing, he cast off several of his illegitimate offspring—those whom he had recognized and admitted into the bosom of his family. He regretted his softness of heart. "I did them wrong by pampering them," he said. "While they were young, well, I could not help it. But when they were old enough to shift for themselves, I should have let them go out on their own, and not soften them by giving them everything they wanted".

The Shylock mask never wore off. You could see it on his King of the *Schnorrers*, his Elisha Ben Abuya. It peered at you in every part he played. But it was not veneer. It was Ritter's true self at last.

When an older man speaks of a graceless adventurer, a spendthrift, a Don Juan, a big-hearted father, a patron of the falling and the failing, he means the early Ritter. The new generation, in the period of the decay of the Yiddish theatre—which Ritter lived to see—points to the ungrateful actor, the selfish and avaricious man who posed as a proud defender of his people and a believer in ideals, but whose impersonation of Shylock which was a vindication of his people was played only on the stage. The real Shylock had settled in his bones. When his arteries began to harden, the blood of Shylock congealed in his veins. The mask and the masquerader were fused.

XVI

Manewitz Leaves the Stage

THEY THOUGHT OF DEATH—IF AT ALL—AS A FAR-OFF STATION at the end of a long road. Life was a game, and when Death toppled over one of the players, the rest gave vent to their grief in loud lamentation and show. Their mourning was the ritual of a primitive people. Mourning over, they went back to their play refreshed.

But when Manewitz died it was like a convulsion of nature. What a mighty stroke of the Angel of Death to lay low that giant! He was a symbol of strength and aggression. Mighty stars and managers stood in awe of him. There was no one brave enough to tamper with his scripts. He spoke arrogantly. He disregarded convention and refused to knuckle under for advantage. And now, there he lay, stiffened out, staring sightlessly at the ceiling.

The Yiddish Rialto was overwhelmed. It was felt that there must be a dramatic exhibition of grief worthy of the tragedy. If not now, when? A black-letter day in the annals

213

of the theatre—the day of Manewitz's funeral. Let the or-
chestras play soft music—find the funeral marches and play
them with vigor; let the cellos wail and groan; let the violins
play with muted strings; let the trombones blare. The stage
should be set in black. Put a few gigantic urns near the
footlights on either side. Drape mourning bands from the
top gallery down to the orchestra. Hang his enlarged portrait in the center of the proscenium, and lower it for all
to see. When such a great man dies, art should provide a
performance that fits the occasion.

Let Winchefsky, the grandfather of Yiddish literature in
America, write a series of articles describing the last painful
hours of the deceased (as he did after he returned from his
vacation in the Catskills, much improved by the mountain
air). Don't turn Baranof away; let him also write of his
friendship with Manewitz, who had persuaded him—Baranof, who looked like Beethoven—to compose his twenty-
first symphony. That symphony rests in manuscript, un-
published for lack of funds, but when it is finally published
it will be dedicated to the memory of the great Manewitz.
Joel Antin is entitled to the floor. That erudite journalist
began a series of articles that continued until the first an-
niversary of Manewitz's death. They were articles that exhausted the entire subject; Antin promised that there was
a book to be written. That promise is yet to be fullfilled.
The resplendent Ritter cannot be denied the right to his
word; he calls his secretary and dictates an article of reminiscences about Manewitz; of course, the secretary will fill in
the details; you may be sure he will write the article to
Ritter's satisfaction; and you may also be sure that he will
avoid all references to the contracts broken by Ritter, to
the royalties Ritter didn't pay.

What Manewitz had given to the Yiddish theatre was the

burden of this outpouring of mourning. He had written a large number of plays—about forty in all. Many of them were not original. He had taken suggestions from the dramas of all theatres. He had rewritten operettas and farces, and adapted well-known plays by giving them a Jewish slant. He had paraphrased, in a Jewish setting, the best of Hauptmann's tragic plays, and he had transplanted dozens of the works of leading Russian dramatists. But there was always integrity in his workmanship. His dialogue was sensible and interesting. His wit was not of the theatre, but in character drawing. It was said that he wrote plays to order. So did Shakespeare. So did every dramatist who made the writing of plays a profession. And writing plays became Manewitz's profession. In short, he was the ablest man of letters the Yiddish theatre had acquired. The repertoire of all acting companies was based on Manewitz's work. His plays were the foundation of Madame Lessin's career—in "Mirele Efros," the Jewish opposite of "King Lear;" in "Die Shevuah," the reverse of Hauptmann's "Fuhrmann Heschel;" in "Die Shechita," based on a sketch by Peretz; in "Rosa Brandt," Hauptmann's play; in "Lucrezia Borgia," adapted from Victor Hugo. Burlak would have been a mere wind-bag of an actor if he had not played in Manewitz's "The Charlatan," and "The Kreutzer Sonata," and together with Madame Lessin in all her plays. Ritter never would have achieved his position in the theatre had it not been for Manewitz's "King Lear," a paraphase of Shakespeare's play; his "Der Fremder," his "Elisha Ben Abuya" and "Der Meturef." Nor did he write plays only for the stars. They were all good ensemble plays. In them every actor in the company was given an opportunity. The character player could distinguish himself, and likewise the villain and the comedian. He had a kind heart also for the ordinary people

of the union, and seldom wrote a play in which there was
no place for the chorus men and the chorus women; and
he had no objection, later on, if a song were introduced and
the orchestra could be employed. He felt that the entire
theatre had to be fed, and he was the mother feeding them
with good parts and with opportunities for service. This
was the gist of what they wrote about him in the press and
at memorial meetings, and every scribbler who had ever
said "hello" to Manewitz in a coffee-house took pen in hand
and wrote personal reminiscences and anecdotes to his
heart's content. Their eulogies oozed with praise; of the
dead nothing but good should be spoken; don't be stingy!

The actors' union gave form to its sentiments in long
resolutions. Black bands were ordered worn on the sleeves
of all members. The vulgar operettas were laid aside; there
was a cycle of "serious" plays; "Broken Hearts" written by
the sentimentalist Krolik, was revived, and added to the
flood of tears.

There was no mistaking the fact that the Yiddish theatre
was in mourning. Manewitz's death ended a chapter. The
curtain had fallen on the last act of the last play. A new
chapter in the history of the theatre would have to be written. Who were to be the authors, the designers, the pro-
ducers, and who were to act in the plays that would be
registered in that chapter? Until a reply was forthcoming,
let mourning have full sway.

The grief of one man was unnoticed. He was a silent
mourner. They called him Kemat. He was a stout little fellow with a nose like a ferret's. He pretended not to know
what was going on in the world except what related to
Manewitz. That was his work. He was the guardian of
Manewitz's plays. He knew the quality of the playwright's
genius and was its slave. He was in quick succession a ped-

dler, a scene-shifter, an usher; and then, accidentally hearing one of Manewitz's plays in rehearsal, his ears were pierced for life. He became the slave of Manewitz's plays. When Manewitz wanted to know anything about his properties, so to speak—who would play what, what they owed him, what was going on in the theatre, how many actors were used in this or that play—he sent for Kemat.

He first acquired the habit of using Kemat for errands. Then he proposed having him sleep in the house. It was a sweeping gesture of hospitality. "Let room be found for Kemat!" There were seven children and six rooms. "Give him a place in the garret," he said to his wife, a woman with mournful eyes. "Treat him like one of the family," he added sternly. She vanished into the kitchen. All right to argue with the grocer or butcher, but not with the tyrant whom fate had assigned as her provider.

"Mr. Manewitz," said Kemat one day, "it's shameful how they cheat you."

"They are rogues," said Manewitz.

"But what robbers!" said Kemat. "They falsify their books. They play three times and pay for one. They should be watched."

"Then why don't you catch them?" asked Manewitz.

Kemat thus became the collector of his royalties. Not being a bookkeeper, he kept the accounts in his head. He watched the posters and the advertisements in the press, and prowled around the theatres. He was there with his reckoning on pay day, and would not go away unsatisfied, even if he had to follow the manager home. He knew all of Manewitz's plays—how many times they had been played, the intake of each play in terms of royalties, how many characters in each, what stage business had been invented without Manewitz's authority, and who were the saboteurs.

At the height of his success, Manewitz's body filled out.

His bank account became respectable. He owned a house in Brooklyn. Manewitz complained of illness and had a doctor visit him. A ripple of anxiety spread through all the coffee-houses frequented by the acting fraternity. X-rays were taken, medicine prescribed. Manewitz was ordered to bed. He refused to remain for long, dressed himself, and went about the streets as usual. When the pain returned, he sent for another doctor, and it was discovered that it was a serious matter. There were ulcers in his stomach. Then there were ominous whispers that it might be cancer. A shudder rippled through the coffee-houses. Manewitz felt the wings of the Angel of Death brush his cheek. And when they covered him that night, he looked at those who were nursing him with a strange interest. Then they had to give him morphine to dull the pain. It confused his thoughts and deranged his vision. When he was bundled to bed and saw his trousers on a hanger, he wondered sadly whether his body would ever fill them again. He lingered for months on a sick bed. He looked like an ox whose vitals were being gnawed at by an invisible monster. He hadn't the strength to throw it off. He felt it was useless to fight, it was useless to think. So he turned his face to the wall, and closed his eyes; he stretched out and death came as a relief.

Kemat witnessed the tragedy. He walked about the streets, into the home; he made inquiries and went away. His eyes were red, and he did not eat for days. When they mentioned cancer, he was thrown into great excitement.

"Don't tell me he has cancer," he shouted. Even when Manewitz's body was laid out on the floor and covered with a sheet, he rejected the diagnosis.

"He was sick and tired of living. But just when he was feeling at peace with the world—when his family had food, he had money in his pocket—he was stabbed in the back.

You read it in the vile sheet which printed the articles that
killed him. Who wrote them? It was not an enemy. It was
his best friend, who gets all of a sudden an idea that he
must begin to tell the truth, and to tell the truth he must
compare Manewitz with Ibsen, Manewitz with Shakespeare,
and being a candid friend, he had to admit that Manewitz
was an imitator, a plagiarist, a hack writer, and that he even
stole scenes from his own plays. Did you ever hear the like?
Tell the truth about anybody and there'll be nothing left
of his character. The whole world would be destroyed by
truth. All his life Manewitz told just enough of the truth to
enable the world to live. All his life he fought like a bear.
He prized loyalty and friendship and fought for friends,
but when he saw his friend stick a dagger in his back, he
did not care to fight any more. He gave it up. He made
up his mind to die, and when he made up his mind, not
all the East Side doctors could make it different. There
was no use arguing with him."

Indeed, Manewitz was beyond the reach of argument,
especially any argument that Kemat could advance.

So let us return to the stage where the memorial services
were being conducted. It was crowded with celebrities from
uptown and downtown—with labor leaders and intelligentsia, settlement workers and artists, all of them dressed in
black. Near the dressing-room, in a corner, Kemat found a
seat. He could see the backs of the speakers and was saved
the pain of hearing them. His eyes were hot and dry. He
tried to get near the Manewitz family, buf they were on the
other side of the stage; they had no part to play in the
exercise, except as mourners, to weep copiously. Kemat went
through the back entrance and took the subway to the
cemetery. Again, at the grave, there was a crowd through

which he could not break; he bent down, tried to see what was going on through the legs of the fortunate ones gathered around the hole in the ground. He caught a glimpse of the coffin being lowered. He moved from one end of the circle to the other, trying to break through the crowd of men and women, but it was impossible. He felt like crying out loud to give expression to the physical pain he felt when the body was lowered, but his throat was closed and his lips would not move. The mob pressed against him and shoved him away from the grave.

Kemat was alone in his grief. His world had come to an end but he had to keep on living in it. He left New York for a shack in the Catskills near Fallsburg, where he spent the summer. When he returned, it seemed as if time had stopped for him. He was unshaven, his clothes were dirty and ragged. He could barely drag his legs, and his eyes were heavy with sleep. He was seeking familiar scenes, but the absence of one face made them all look strange and unfamiliar.

He found himself in Marcus's café, listening to the murmur of conversation. His ears were strained to hear the name of Manewitz. They were talking of the theatre. The actors' union threatened a strike. Ritter had met the threat by suggesting that he would retire from the stage or make a tour of South America. Burlak was going to open the season with a new play by Lecker. Madame Lessin had a wonderful play that had come to her, it was said, via Madame Duse. A newspaper man said that the dramatist of the new season was to be Leon Grobyan. Another threw Krolik's hat in the ring. They had forgotten Manewitz.

Kemat wandered through the streets of the East Side. He did not enjoy the autumn smells, the bustle of preparation for the holidays, the eager faces of businessmen rushing about, satisfied that it was to be a good season. The reference to Grobyan inspired a thought. Perhaps there was a way for him to remain with the theatre. He found Grobyan in an apartment on Second Avenue, dismembering a herring with his fingers and stopping his thirst with tea. The room was in disorder. Grobyan's wife quickly shoved several children into another room and disappeared with them.

Still eating with relish, Grobyan motioned with his head to Kemat to take a seat.

"What are you doing here, Kemat?" he inquired.

"Then you know me," exclaimed Kemat.

"You damn fool, who doesn't know you?" growled Grobyan.

Encouraged by this friendly reception, Kemat said:

"You know, I have been with Manewitz for fifteen years, and he was always satisfied with me. All of his plays I know, who has them, who plays them, and how often."

"Of course, your occupation is gone, my friend," said Grobyan. "There won't be any more playing of Manewitz. You will have to get yourself a new job."

"That's the idea. Maybe I could do for you what I did for Manewitz," said Kemat, eagerly.

"You could not do better for yourself. I have written God knows how many plays—most of them are good, some are even better," said Grobyan, "and now that Manewitz is dead, who but I am his natural successor, and my plays will be in great demand this season."

"I could collect your royalties," said Kemat, "and, more than that, I would watch them. I wouldn't let them play any tricks with your plays. These purse-snatchers must be watched."

"That would never do," said Grobyan, alarmed. "When I sell a play, it is sold; lock, stock and barrel it belongs to the manager. It is because my plays don't bother me after I sell them that I enjoy life."

Kemat looked at Grobyan sadly, and took his hat. He was in the wrong place after all. A theatre led by Grobyan was not to his liking.

"A shoemaker, that's what you are," he muttered and made for the door.

Grobyan heard him, pushed the dishes away, and moved toward him.

"You're an impudent rascal," he shouted. "Comes to my house and calls me a shoemaker. Let me tell you that Manewitz's plays are as dead as he is. Those tedious plays he wrote were stolen from God knows who. If anyone wants to play them now, they will have to be revamped and adapted and remade."

"Who is there that dares do that?" asked Kemat, looking back through the door.

"The greatest Yiddish dramatist of this century—that's me," yelled Grobyan, as Kemat disappeared.

He was right. They never played Manewitz's plays again, as they were originally written. Scenes were mangled or omitted, words exchanged, endings altered. It was a free country. The plays were never the same again.

"An ungrateful world," muttered Kemat. "It's bitter to live."

The portrait of Manewitz, in a gilded frame, hangs in every Yiddish theatre. In the club-rooms of the actors' union his big, bulging eyes look down upon the habitués as they play pinochle or poker, exchange scandal and smoke cigarettes. In every book written on the Yiddish theatre they devote a chapter to Manewitz. His name is mentioned at banquets. Joseph Barondess always arranges an annual banquet in his memory, and delivers a eulogy of the great dramatist. There was a man for you. Scenes that touched the heart. You could weep and you could cry. Words that had sense. He had a philosophy of his own. What was it? Don't be a *shegetz*. Read Joel Antin's articles that have been bound in a volume, and he'll tell you. But he had every-thing—comedy, tragedy, ideals, problems. He was a man of the theatre. He made the theatre what it is. His was the master mind. This was the make-believe on parade.

But Kemat knew what was in their hearts. Pretense! They preferred Grobyan's melodramas because there was money in them. They liked Krolik's feeble stories for they had tears in them and the public paid dearly for the satisfaction of weeping. They preferred the plays yokels came to see, for there were more yokels in the world than philosophers. Manewitz's words—those thick juicy words about which they would often brag in his lifetime—gave the actors a headache to memorize, and besides, why should the public think of the playwright when there were actors who were dying for applause and appreciation?

Kemat sees them pass into the theatre. He hears what they say when they leave after the performance. He listens to the off-stage views of the actors. They can't bluff him. He knows them all. He shakes his fist at them and mutters:

"Hypocrites! Swine! He gave you his life, left you pearls, and you wallow in *shund!*"

XVII

Kenia Lessin in Retirememt

SHE HAD PASSED THROUGH THE FIRES OF LIFE AND NOW LIVED in the glow of its dying embers. Echoes and shadows filled her days. There were memories of a hungry childhood; memories of violent passion; echoes of applause in the theatre; dark hours of pain and tragedy; and then a long stretch of boredom. Now the frail and faltering figure was a mere storehouse of experiences blurred by time. Her best moments were in the routine of the day or night—eating, dozing, walking in the near-by park, hearing an old tune, seeing something fresh and bright. Something was left of the warmth of mere living. She hated to talk of the past. Once she had loved to win at cards, now she was unable to tell one card from another. She listened to the radio, but the programs were confusing.

Once a year she appeared in an old play. She was unable to remember the lines of her part, nor was she quick enough to catch the cues from the prompter. They loved

224

to see her on the stage, regardless of her playing. She still moved with stateliness in "Mirele Efros," as she had for years, but the stays she wore were fatiguing, and she loved to settle down in a negligee, in a comfortable rocker near the window. She could smell the geraniums boxed on the sill. The breeze would often bring the perfume of lilacs from the near-by park. She had never had any children of her own, but she loved to hear the prattle of children.

She was living too long. These years were an epilogue she could have dispensed with. Death was reluctant to strike her down with one strong blow. She was being reduced bit by bit. Here she was—Death's living captive, looking both ways at the same time—at Life receding and at Death looming in the distance.

That was not how the magnificent Ritter had been taken off the stage. His body had begun to creak. He had been seeing physicians and taking medicines. Death struck him suddenly, and with one blow reduced him to a crumpled pulp of a man. He gave up the struggle with a grand gesture. He made his exit with a flourish. He was always the actor.

It was in far-off Odessa that she met him. She was young and eager. The village where she was born was only a few miles from the great city. After her mother died, when her stepfather had approached her with peculiar gestures, she fled to the city. She ran like a young animal to preserve her life. She became a servant in a brothel, where Ritter found her. He took her out of surroundings she found barely endurable. She looked up to him as a god who had freed her. It was her first real experience in life. It was her pulsating springtime. She gave herself to him with a prodigality that disturbed him. He brought her to the theatre and showed her the unreal world, the world of sham, of artifice, of pretense. Through him she became a woman and an actress. She became Kenia Lessin. That was the name she made her own, shared with no one—an unchanging name that is still remembered.

Many of the Yiddish players, expelled from Rumania or Russia, went directly to New York. Some lacked the strength to make the journey in one leap. They detoured to London as a temporary refuge. They found a Jewish community lingering in poverty, living in appalling slums, doing their best to be at home; but the climate and the people were alien. The theatre the players used was a drafty building, and there was no money for stage settings or bright lights. They had a sordid existence. Not even the restaurants in Whitechapel were warm or congenial; they were always too cold or too damp.

When she arrived with Ritter in London, they were on terms of friendship. He was free and easy. His amours ranged from matrons to servants in the house; from the courtesans at the Pavilion to women plying their trade in Piccadilly. She did not mind. She had lost the freshness and eagerness of youth. She was capable of great physical endurance. She had acquired a talent for simulating hysteria. She was no longer illiterate, although reading was an effort for her to the end of her days. She memorized her parts by having them read to her. But on the stage she came to life in a strange, clairvoyant way. There, she lived every moment and gave to her impersonations an intensity few Yiddish players possessed.

She remembered the day when she realized for the first time that Ritter had become a stranger. She did not mind the frowzy brunette he brought with him to the café rendezvous. He was as affable and clever as always, but she could not endure to see him laugh with gusto at the crude observations of his partner of the evening. Once she had broken with him, she was free to carry on affairs of her own. It seemed that she was no longer capable of sustained affections or passions. They flared up quickly, and as quickly cooled.

She remembered London scenes only vaguely. She was unable to learn English, but clung to Russian and Yiddish. She seldom went to the London theatres. She remembered a few restaurants in Piccadilly—a kosher restaurant in Ward-our Street, which reminded her of the fish smells of Odessa. Once she was taken to Kensington Park, but it rained that afternoon. Once she heard an opera in Covent Garden. She was a transient in the great metropolis.

She left London for New York, alone. She joined a company playing in the Rumanian Opera House near Astor Place. It was a gloomy theatre. Not being able to sing or dance, she could take only serious parts, which she played with mild success. To her great surprise, Ritter soon joined the company and many others came along, landing in what was to be their last station. The New York Ghetto was lively and increasing in size, and soon there were thousands filling the three theatres. The Jewish workingmen in the tenements were being organized. The Socialist movement became strong, loud, and vulgar. The audiences were rough, indulgent, and familiar in the theatre. They loved to see the old life brought back in the theatre, to hear an old song, to be reminded of the Jewish past. They still remembered the *shtetl*. It was an audience it was easy to play to.

Here the talent of Kenia Lessin ripened, and with the advent of Manewitz she became the possessor of a repertoire of plays in which her parts, portraying old or young women, stood out in bold relief and enabled her to dominate the stage. With the Jews' usual exaggeration of what they love, she was likened to Duse and Bernhardt. She tried to live up to her reputation by not appearing in operettas or farces or melodramas. She was not easy to please. She chose her own plays and played her own parts, and rejected anything that did not measure up to her high position.

And she lived alone. It seemed to her now that she had always lived alone. She had her own apartment, her own partners at cards, and a few friends who sat at her table in Zeitlen's restaurant. Her affairs with men did not monopolize her time or thought. She had become, in a sense, conventional. Something in her had died after Ritter broke with her, and it never returned. She had left her youth in Odessa. She liked to have young people around her, but she never felt young again herself.

She had followers who idolized her. Among them was Belvon, who brought with him from Russia a noisy enthusiasm for the theatre. When he saw Madam Lessin for the first time, he was sure that she was a star of the first magnitude, and he would worship at no other shrine in the Yiddish theatre. All the others had no talent. She had to admit that he was never unfaithful to that first enthusiasm, and for the rest of his life, whatever their relations, she was always the peer of Duse. Fortunately for him, his love for the theatre was shared with a material interest in a Yiddish newspaper, of which he was the publisher. He might have remained a distant adorer, but a newspaper controversy opened the stage door to Belvon.

A venal editor had gone out of his way to attack Belvon's great star. This miscreant, who spent his leisure time drinking and gambling and fornicating, thought it would help circulation to become the defender of the purity of family life. The "Tageblatt" was an orthodox publication. He owed it to his readers to check the licentiousness of the stage, especially that of the writings of Manewitz and of Madame Lessin, who appeared in them. He went at it hammer and tongs. Every new play was the target of a series of denunciations.

It was not Belvon's business to take up the cudgels for Manewitz. He himself was able to tear Manewitz's plays to shreds, to tell where he got his plots and how those fine Russian plays were mangled in adaptation. But Madame Lessin could not be left undefended. Circulation was also a matter of some importance too. He hated Paley. He hated the "Tageblatt." He was a lover of the best in the theatre. His raging heart did not let him rest, so he became Madame Lessin's defender, and this got him to know his favorite actress well. When she found herself with a protector, Madame Lessin was gratified and showed it with great skill. Belvon was bewildered by her attentions. He lost himself in a welter of art and passion and business. Finally, she ended his misery by marrying him according to the laws of Moses.

For the first time she knew what it meant to be a married woman and domesticated, although Belvon was not a religious man, belonged to no congregation or fraternal society, was a partisan of no cause. He was the publisher of a newspaper and had to maintain certain social amenities, in spite of the fact that he loved the theatre, gambling, and various shady amusements. He himself was disreputable, but his paper was respectable and he did his best to keep within limits.

She remembered how gradually she moved from the center near the Thalia and found herself in a little bandbox theatre on the Bowery, three or four blocks uptown. Her friends came to the theatre to see her and not the plays.

.

It would have been a lucrative business but for the unions. All the specifications the unions had invoked for the larger theatres applied in a measure also to Madame Lessin's theatre, where no supers were needed, where you could get along without music, no scene-shifters were required, where two or three ushers could serve instead of eight. Belvon's life was absorbed in endless disputes with the actors and the unions. They reduced his profits to the vanishing point. By this time his newspaper had passed into bankruptcy, and his sole interest became the management of his wife's affairs. He made weekend trips to neighboring theatres, and in that way his losses in New York were balanced by his profits in Newark, New Haven, and Philadelphia; but the sheriff was always just around the corner.

Under these circumstances Madame Lessin and Belvon were living under the formal terms of marriage. Their disputes made up the larger part of their common existence. These usually centered on the problem of her "jewels." She always believed in having something tucked away in her stocking. What was there was an accumulation over the years of valuable jewels, which she regarded as her life insurance. When the season seemed about to dry up, Belvon began making the usual approaches to the "jewels." He would groan and threaten and shout and prove how much he had lost in the theatre. Then he would disappear for days and finally show up at the theatre with bleary eyes, hair disheveled and a wild glare of despair, waiting for the proper moment again to spring the suggestion that all he needed to save his life was the temporary loan of the "jewels." Time and again she let him have the "jewels." Time and again he brought them back to her.

But what was it on that spring day that prompted her to repulse him and refuse the favor of the loan? She could not remember clearly. His presence on that day, when the smell of the flowers came into the apartment, was profane and repulsive. She could not endure the thought of continuing this repetitious farce endlessly—playing every night, playing matinees, crossing by ferry to a neighboring city, always with the same repertoire, always with the same lack of means to carry the enterprise to the end of the season. The next season would be like the last. The next year would be like the one before. And he would be getting meaner in appearance, more dissipated, while she would find it ever harder to go through the routine of life, always wanting more rest and having to work harder. It was unbearable.

So, the day he asked for the "jewels," she shouted back at him, "You cannot have them—no!"

He stood there as if he did not understand what she meant, and then he turned away and left the apartment. That same evening he came to the theatre and seemed cool and self-possessed. He had sent flowers to be placed on her dressing-table. He said that the house was filled. He arranged to meet her at the restaurant after the performance. Then he said, softly:

"What has come over you? Dozens of times you gave me the 'jewels' to pawn. Every time I brought them back to you. The sheriff is at my throat; I must put my hands on money, do you hear? Give me the jewels!"

She laughed. It was the hysterical laughter of one of her plays. In that play she had played the part of a young girl married to a much older man, and driven to insanity by their relations. Twice in the play she gave expression to the wildest hysteria. It was always one of her most remarkable impersonations. Here, facing Belvon, she gave an exclamation of mockery. She would not give in to him this time. To make her do so he would have had to shake her—

slap her face, beat her—but he did nothing of the sort. He
looked at her as if he saw in her eyes something he had
never before suspected. What was he thinking of? He could
not have been thinking of that young man upon whom she
had smiled, and who had smiled back at her. Her rendezvous had been discreetly arranged. It must have been the
business of the theatre, losses every week. The people just
would not come into the theatre. It was obvious that the
new play was a failure. She had warned him, but he would
not listen to her. Her refusal to deliver the "jewels" at his
command was her perverse way of telling him that had he
listened to her, they would have taken the other play and
there would have been no need to pawn the jewels.

He came close to her, grasped her by the shoulders,
glared down at her, and cried out again. "Don't you understand? I don't know where to turn. Give me the jewels, or
by God Almighty, I will shoot myself right here and now!"

This was too much. She could no longer control herself. She looked at him. He was not the husky animal he
had been when she married him. Gambling and a slovenly
life had used him up. His face often flushed and then became alarmingly pale; his jaw drooped; his hatreds and
passions had consumed him. His body had long since fallen
far behind his temperament; his blood was still hot, but his
blood-vessels might burst at any moment, suffocating his
heart.

She was determined not to please him. She had to have it
out with him. If he could now bully her into acquiescence,
then that was the end of her freedom. He would always be
able to have his way. She threw a bottle of cologne at the
mirror and pieces of glass scattered over her dressing-table.

"Don't you threaten me," she cried. "You want the
'jewels' to pay a gambling debt, or to buy a fur coat for

that slattern who hangs around you. I've told you for the last time, you can't have them now and you can't have them tomorrow. You will never see those jewels. Look out for yourself. I am tired of being your banker."

He gasped and fell back, leaning against the closet where her many costumes were kept. He spat. It seemed to her, looking at him through the mirror, that he was thinking of something to say that would express the depth of his loathing. Instead, he stood up and said, "I am going right out of here and I am going to kill myself at your door."

"Don't give me any of your melodrama," she cried, her anger rising. "You don't know how to live like a man and you haven't got the courage to die like a man."

"Have it your way," he muttered, and turned to the door.

And so it happened. He walked out of the room and slammed the door. It seemed that only a few moments elapsed. She heard some shuffling on the other side of the door. She heard a shot. Then there seemed to be a long silence. The door opened and there he lay with blood streaming down his face, out of his mouth, over his shirt, and a crowd pressing around him. She felt an agonizing pain, and for the first time in her life she gave way to an unfeigned hysteria, which seemed to carry her out of the theatre through crowded noisy streets, into her apartment with a doctor and nurses holding her down, drenching her with medicines and compresses. How long she lay in a state of mental confusion, she never knew.

When she recovered, it seemed as if the whole world had become quiet and orderly. Her hearing was affected. She was excluded from the theatre. For years she was regarded by the Rialto with an uneasy curiosity. She did not know what they were thinking of her. If they spoke to her at all, it was only of conventional matters. Later, to her great surprise, a smiling young man returned her "jewels." She did not remember when she had given them to him. She had forgotten him and the whole incident. The proceeds of the sale of the jewels enabled her to settle down without being dependent upon anyone. It was the end of the tragedy. The last act was being prolonged. The *held* had passed away. Death was giving her a reprieve. She was living on borowed time. She was not to be taken at once. She often wondered whether it would not have been better if she had used the revolver and Belvon had been condemned to have his days prolonged. It would have served him right.